*J. M. Alden*

FOR FORTY YEARS EDITOR OF HARPER'S MAGAZINE

# MAGAZINE WRITING

## AND

# THE NEW LITERATURE

*259*

BY

HENRY MILLS ALDEN, Litt.D., LL.D.

AUTHOR OF
"GOD IN HIS WORLD" AND "A STUDY OF DEATH"

HARPER & BROTHERS PUBLISHERS
NEW YORK AND LONDON
MCMVIII

# CONTENTS

## PART I

### THE RELATION OF PERIODICAL TO GENERAL LITERATURE

## PART II

### THE NEW LITERATURE

# CONTENTS

# INTRODUCTION

THE writer of this volume has had two objects in view: First, to show the intimate relations of periodical to general literature, as to authorship and aim; secondly, to present certain characteristic features of a new life and literature, beginning two generations ago, with the emergence, in the natural course of evolution, of the distinctively modern psychical era.

These two objects are closely associated, as periodical literature has, from its earliest to its latest period, not only reflected, but has had a large share in initiating, the successive variations in the general evolution. Our consideration, therefore, while it is not a methodically planned treatise, has a certain unity of purpose. It is limited to the imaginative faculty and sensibility as manifest in the very modern life and literature of England and America, with only such allusions to other races and periods as help to show from what fashions of an older order our modernity is a departure. It is the editor who speaks throughout, but mainly from his experience and observation in the open field here chosen, with little reference to matters directly concerning his own or the contributors' special relations to magazine - making — such matters belonging properly to a wholly different kind of book from that herein undertaken. This volume is made up largely of selections from the "Editor's Study" in *Harper's Magazine*.

In Part First no attempt has been made to give a history of periodical literature. That would require many volumes. Indeed, there is no semblance of a record after 1860—no mention of such important undertakings as *Scribner's*, which afterward became the *Century*, or of the later *Scribner's*, to say nothing of others which, though of brief continuance, were, in their time, notable. This later period is well within the memory of contemporary readers in all its aspects, including the relation to these magazines of all the eminent writers, English and American, for two generations. The earlier period is less known, and has, therefore, received more attention. Since 1860, no distinction, as to quality or as to any substantial values, can be made between the best books and the best periodicals.

More consideration has been given in this volume to life than to literature. Creative genius is manifest in life, in the transformation of human nature and human sensibility, before it is expressed in literary embodiment and interpretation. Imaginative literature is closer to life in our day than it has ever been before, essentially a part of it. Genius, which is only another name for the creative imagination, shaped human life before there was art or literature; and, in the evolution of genius, the variations in æsthetic and psychical sensibility are the same as in all the imaginative creations appealing to that sensibility.

The term evolution and the phraseology applicable to the procedure thus named have come into general use, very well serving their scientific purpose. There is also a general presumption, quite untenable, that the universe is planned, and that evolution is its explanation. Of the real world there is no plan and no explanation. We speak of one form of existence as emerging from a previous form, as if the latest form were thus accounted for. If there were any accounting for anything, it would seem more reasonable to reverse this order and look to the ultimate as accounting for the whole series. The idea of implication, of involution, would tend to occupy our minds to the exclusion of that of explication or evolution. All such terms are notional, due to limitations incident to our mental constitution or habit. The assumption that they express reality, if persisted in, leads us to the conception of a mechanical universe, to a sterile speculation.

Putting aside these notions and accepting the manifestations of life in living terms, we are in a real world. Instead of making formulas and fancying that we are thus explaining things, we behold the reality and take it, in all its inexplicableness.

The formal phrases, "the homogeneous becoming the heterogeneous," "specialization," "the tendency to increased variation at every successive stage," and so on, are translated, and we see life as creative, fertile, abundant, and ever more and more abounding. We take the evil along with the good, making no problem of their reconcilement, since they are elements in a natural solution, and we escape those fantastic labels of "optimist" and "pessimist."

This way of seeing life and of representing it in imaginative literature we call the new realism. By way of contrast, considerable attention has been given to primitive realism, but we trust our self-indulgence in dwelling upon the earliest workings of the human imagination, which have for us a fascination in inverse ratio to any possible definite knowledge of them, may not impose too severe a tax upon the reader's patience. The period separating that old from the new realism is so complex and so vast—covering nearly the whole of human history—that no writer could attempt even a concisely comprehensive treatment. The sophistications abounding in this period have been considered to some extent, also the affectations, pedantries, disguises, pomps, and other antique fashions of life and literature, in order to show how far removed from this unreal investiture is the plainly human guise of life and literature in our own time. But, along with the disclosure of these errancies and distortions there has been ample recognition of the essential values and charms of the old order, whose greatness compels our admiration and whose sincerities, however masked, appeal to our affections.

To some readers it may seem strange that the beginning of the new psychical era and of the new literature should have been given so recent a date as the middle of the last century, and that the finality of the break with the past in the present generation should be so strongly emphasized. So quick and complete a transformation of human nature and sensibility is not easily credited—especially by those who persistently hold that these are in all ages essentially the same. There has, indeed, been nothing added to human nature. It has received no new endowment; but the permissive conditions for this remarkable renascence were almost suddenly apparent, and the change, speedy and radical as it was, seemed natural and inevitable. The Second Part of this volume is devoted entirely to the new psychical era which was ushered in by this quiet renascence, and to its manifestations in life and literature, little reference being made to poetry, because it is in imaginative prose that the unprecedented features disclosed have been developed.

In tracing the evolution of the imagination, the writer has had in view only a clearer indication of the tendencies which distinguish present from past literature. He does not claim that these tendencies have resulted in a greater literature; he has only tried to show wherein it is a new literature—of what traits it has been divested and what is its fresh investiture. In portraying the contrast, he might very easily be misunderstood as framing an indictment against the whole past of humanity, since the salient features of this past, brought out in the contrast, seem to boldly intimate an elaborately extravagant masquerade. The very terms which inevitably suggest themselves for the apt expression of this intimation are those which imply aversion on our part, else they would be untrue to our modern sense of life. But they do not imply either contempt or condemnation. Symbols which are alien to us have had their significance; and what seems to us unreal and even incapable of realization, in any true harmony of life, has been at least relatively real, though in a false perspective. Perversity is not insincerity. It is, from our point of view, quite impossible for us to understand how anybody could ever have been burned alive for heresy; but we need to comprehend even so ghastly a horror as the sequel of an attitude just the opposite of ours. We make allowance for a vast distortion of view, but we are not justified in any attempt at apology; he who would venture to patronize the past convicts himself of folly.

We are not myth-makers, but we can see what an advance myth-making was beyond the primitive naturalism from which it emerged. So with every stage of the evolution—it was an advance; and in every period there are abundant phenomena for our sympathetic interpretation, appealing to our sense of the beautiful and to our admiration. Of our own period, also, we say—it is an advance. As to its attitude, we may say that it is the ultimate advance. What its possibilities are, when this attitude reaches its consummation by a universal acceptance, no one can predict. Present accomplishments are at least interesting enough to pique expectation, at the same time guarding us against the illusory hope of ever again beholding the kind of greatness displayed by the overshadowing might of past exemplars.

Some attention has been given to features distinctive of the new art as well as to those of the new literature—especially in the chapter on "The New Art of Prose." But a special consideration of what is called "the literary art," dealing with technical methods in style and construction, does not properly come within the scope of the present work. Equally foreign to a work treating of purely imaginative values would be the consideration of ethical purpose, except by implication: it being understood that no idealism is consistent with degeneracy.

# PART I

## THE RELATION OF PERIODICAL TO
## GENERAL LITERATURE

# MAGAZINE WRITING
## AND THE NEW LITERATURE

259

## CHAPTER I

### EARLY PERIODICAL LITERATURE

IN the history of literature no subject is more interesting or more pertinent to the whole course of development than that of periodical publication.

Our modern idea of publication is generally confined to the issue and circulation of printed works, excepting in the case of plays that have publicity only as they are acted, and of musical compositions which are known to the general public only as they are rendered by musicians. This exceptional form of publication was the original and only form in the most ancient times, when there was not even the written symbol, and publication was through oral tradition. It is, moreover, the only form which to-day reaches, as it has in all ages reached, the illiterate, transcending, therefore, by direct and universal appeal, the device of written word and of typography. Before these devices existed all speech was simply phonetic, and unembarrassed by orthoepic puzzles and ambiguities.

Such literature as there was before letters—in the martial and religious lyric, the heroic epic, the elementary drama, and the impassioned speech—was closely associated with religious ritual and with regularly recurrent festivals, themselves following the routine of nature in days, seasons, years, and lustres, and was therefore to a large extent periodical in its communication to the people. The earliest folk-lore and poetry, as represented in Hesiod's *Works and Days*, were calendary, with near relation to agriculture, which, like the gathering of simples and the magical rites of healing, was carried on with a superstitious regard to the phases of the moon. Probably, as soon as printed publications began to circulate among the people, the most fascinating of periodicals was a kind of farmer's almanac.

We doubtless underestimate the number of readers before the invention of types; and the number was comparatively greater in some periods of ancient culture than at any time in mediæval history before the Renaissance. It must have been so in the time when it could be said that "Of the making of many books there is no end." In Rome, even before the Augustan age, intelligent copyists were numerous. Julius Cæsar, who wrote his *Commentaries* to conciliate political favor, had probably no difficulty in securing for them a sufficiently general circulation to effect his purpose. In the next generation any writer who could command the services of hundreds of well-trained slaves could have put upon the market an edition of his latest work larger than the usual first edition of books issued to-day, and in less time. But for this cheap skilled labor the hand printing-press would have come into use. It would have been as easy to make metal types as to engrave signet-rings.

It was not alone the cheapness of labor that met the ancient literary need. Labor was cheap enough in the fifteenth century when types came into use. But there was at this later date no such abundant supply of intelligent servants who could read and write as that derived from the great body of slaves in the palmiest days of the Roman Empire. It was largely due to the intelligence and fidelity of this ingeniously efficient class, whose dependent condition was its misfortune (as in the case of captives taken in battle), rather than its fault, that the stability of the empire was so long maintained, despite the unworthiness of its masters.

The mediæval monks were copyists, and there was a host of them; but they hardly served the interests of a free literature; they were not likely to copy the works of Chaucer, Dante, Petrarch, or Boccaccio, whatever share they may have had in the preservation of classic lore, which was almost entirely Latin.

Printing was a forced invention, rendered necessary rather by the illiteracy of craftsmen than by the demand of a large reading class. In fact, it was printing that first created any considerable general demand for books.

In this situation, which lasted for a century and a half after the invention of the printing-press, there was no call for periodical publications or even for newspapers. There was, indeed, no publication of anything to the people except in the ancient sense— through recitation, oration, the rubric and stage representation. The earliest newspaper printed in Europe was the *Frankfurter Journal*, a weekly, in 1615. A year after the landing of the *Mayflower* followed a similar publication in London, called the *Weekly News*, and not until more than seventy years later was there an English daily paper. Caxton had printed books at Westminster more than two centuries earlier—an interval stretching from the Wars of the Roses to the Revolution of 1688, including the mighty literature produced by the great Elizabethan dramatists, with Shakespeare at their head, by More and Bacon and Sir Thomas Browne, by Spenser and Milton and Bunyan. Yet in all this glorious period no daily newspaper! The English language had come of age. Constitutional liberty, in theory at least, had been achieved. Yet for the great mass of the English people, lacking manhood suffrage, and having no direct responsibility for the conduct of public affairs, there had been developed no regular and organized channels of political expression.

The formation of something which may properly be called public opinion and the establishment of means for its expression rapidly progressed during the closing years of the seventeenth century, so that in 1703 daily journalism became a successful venture. Then began the era of the brilliant and effective publicist in England, nearly a century before there was anything like it on the Continent.

There had been masterly pamphleteering as early as the middle of the seventeenth century, the most eminent examples of which were from the pen of John Milton, mainly in the service of the Commonwealth. This method of appealing to intelligent public opinion was the only one possible at that time, and it was pursued with still greater vigor after the advent of the daily press, because of the constantly increasing number of readers. Defoe and Swift showered pamphlets upon the British nation; but these distinguished writers with even more zest availed of the larger opportunities afforded by periodical publications. Probably no one man ever wielded the power of the press with such effect as Swift did in the *Examiner* during the time of his connection with it.

Defoe had, in 1704, started a periodical of his own, *The Review*, he being at the time a political prisoner in Newgate. He contributed all the matter—essays on politics and commerce—himself, and supplemented each number, of which three were published every week, with "The Scandalous Club," dealing with manners and morals—a precursor of the *Tatler* and *Spectator*, which appeared soon afterward. His *Robinson Crusoe*, after its remarkable success in book form, was published serially in *Heathcote's Intelligencer*, being the first instance of a feuilleton on record. The same fortune—that is, serial after book publication—happened in the next century to Thomson's *Seasons* and to Gray's Elegy. We have witnessed such a reversal of the usual sequence even in our own time in the case of several successful novels, some of which were originally published serially in first-class magazines, then in book form, and again as newspaper feuilletons. As in the case of *Robinson Crusoe*, these later instances indicate the diverse strata of an author's possible audience and help to explain the ever-increasing variety of periodicals.

The intimate association with the earliest periodicals of two such writers as Defoe and Swift, the authors of the two most popular tales not only of their own but of all time, has had its counterpart in every subsequent period of English and American literature. Dryden was the last of the illustrious writers since Chaucer who were denied such association, for though in his last days he was a frequenter of Will's Coffee-House, he did not live quite long enough to witness the triumph of coffee-house literature in the *Tatler*, *Spectator*, and *Guardian*, to which Addison, Steele, Swift, and Pope were contributors.

Before the eighteenth century a writer, however great, who did not produce plays could not depend upon literature for a livelihood. By *The Beggar's Opera*, Gay made more than seven thousand pounds, while the "exquisite" Herrick, though he wrote immortal verse, would have starved but for the living of Dean Prior, given him by Charles I. Sufficient influence at court, or the substantial aid of an aristocratic patron, was necessary to enable the writer to pursue literature at all, and the politic conciliation of such favors involved corresponding obligations and sometimes humiliating compromises. The stage alone afforded profit, with comparative independence, and the widest possible publicity. Yet the ribald public at the time of the Restoration was an exacting tyrant, demanding of playwrights something worse than political accommodation—the prostitution of their art to a corrupted taste. Even Dryden, originally a Puritan, in the early period of his career as a dramatist submitted as supinely as Gay did to this degradation.

The dependence upon royal favor and political patronage was even more extensive in the eighteenth century, because there was a larger number of brilliant writers, whose wit and versatile talent were of such avail and so necessary to party leaders that the obligation was mutual and so equal that it lost its sting. Of all the postulants for official favor, writers like Addison must have been the most independent, such service as they rendered being genial and engaging their eager enthusiasm. Politics was the polite art of the time, and polite literature was willingly subservient to it, but never so absorbed by the service as to diminish its equally alluring offices in the cause of polite criticism and polite manner's, which occupied a large proportion of space in the coffee-house periodicals. Here it was that Addison's critical appreciation of Milton established for his generation a just estimate of the old poet; but it was contemporary letters, as everything else contemporary, that chiefly engrossed attention in an age which, taking itself rather seriously in a stately fashion, is looked back upon as itself an elegant comedy, witty, satirical, and gayly self-complacent.

The *Tatler*, *Spectator*, and a hundred other publications of a like character, though most of these were political rather than literary, which sprang up before Johnson started his short-lived *Rambler*, a generation later, had the polite town for audience, including the women of society. The urban limitation was due to the urbanity of the literature. There was a considerable reading public in England to whom this kind of literature did not appeal, who were readers of Bunyan, and whose chief inducement to learn to read at all was a religious rather than any worldly motive. The interest in politics among the people was, as it had long been, keener and more general in England than in any other land. It was still largely met by tracts and pamphlets, but in the latter half of the century it was stimulated and abundantly nourished by the press. In no other country had there been established so many excellent schools, endowed with special reference to indigent students, for whom ample provision was made, unless they happened to be of Roman Catholic parentage. But elegant literature flourished only in London, or in such fashionable resorts as Bath and Deal, which in this regard, as in their social aspects, but reflected the lustre of the metropolis.

The best essays of the early part of the century, those of the *Spectator* type, seem to us extremely modern rather than modish—modish as that time was. Simple and idiomatic in expression, they were quite free from the artificialities and affectations of contemporaneous verse. They sounded a new note, and had a lasting influence upon all subsequent English literature. Excepting as an instance of striking precocity, we do not wonder that Mrs. Elizabeth Montagu, the "Queen of the Blues," had before her ninth year copied the whole of the *Spectator*. In few novels of our time is there so much of genuine character-making as there is in many of these essays. From Addison's "Sir Roger de Coverley" and "Willy Wimble," and Steele's memoir of "Dick Eastcourt," it is but a step to the novels of Richardson and Fielding.

We also easily pass from the periodicals which published these essays to the earliest type of a monthly magazine, appealing to a general audience through miscellaneous contributions in prose and verse. The germ of this type was Peter Motteux's the *Gentleman's Journal*, established in 1691; but there was no complete or successful example of it until Edward Cave, under the name of "Sylvanus Urban, Gent.," established the *Gentleman's Magazine* about a quarter of a century after Steele started the *Tatler*. This magazine was continuously published for more than one hundred and seventy-five years.

Cave, whose publishing house at St. John's Gate was also his residence, offered prizes for poems on themes suggested by him—as high as £50 for the best on, say, such a subject as "Life, Death, Judgment, Heaven, and Hell." "Sylvanus Urban" had no literary distinction, and by all accounts was not especially "urbane"; but he succeeded in making a successful miscellany, one of the most striking features of which was the reporting of parliamentary debates—a novelty in the journalism of that time.

The fame of the magazine had reached Samuel Johnson at Lichfield, where he had instituted an academy; and when, a few years later, he, with David Garrick, his most promising pupil, went to London to try his fortunes there in the literary field, St. John's Gate was to him like the candle to the moth, and he was used, shyly and afar off, to gaze upon the somewhat stately portal with the deepest

*Novel*

reverence. In 1738 he became the coadjutor of Mr. Cave. Doctor Johnson was thus the first eminent literary man to become closely associated with a popular monthly magazine. Popular it might well be called for those days, having, according to Doctor Johnson, a sale of ten thousand copies. The *Spectator* in its best days, before its first series was paralyzed by the stamp tax of 1712, had a circulation of only three thousand.

The population of London at this time was six hundred thousand. How small a part of this was included in what may be called the polite town may be inferred from the limited audience which Addison addressed, but still more significantly from the fact that theatrical representations reached only about twelve thousand. It was therefore a feather in Johnson's cap that he brought the circulation of Cave's magazine (1740–43) up to fifteen thousand by his version of the current "Parliamentary Debates," which was largely a work of the imagination, since, while he gave the veritable substance, he clothed it in his own magniloquent language. Cave celebrated his good-fortune, according to Hawkins, "by buying an old coach and a pair of older horses." Johnson's tender conscience, when he learned that the parliamentary speeches were taken for genuine, led him to discontinue their publication.

Light literature could hardly be expected from a magazine conducted by either Mr. Cave or Doctor Johnson; indeed, it is only within our own memory that the antiquarian features of this periodical were set aside; but it was lighter than could be found in any other miscellany of the time, and within its first years it had a score of imitators.

Thus was the monthly magazine, which has been for nearly two hundred years one of the most characteristic features of English literature, auspiciously started upon its career.

Periodical literature, in its very beginning, accomplished for the writer one very important result. It enabled him to secure at least partial independence of patronage without recourse to play-writing. The novel, which was its natural offspring, and which, from the first, was a profitable undertaking, helped to complete the emancipation. Richardson's *Pamela*, the earliest society novel, tedious as it may seem to us, appealed to the sympathies of every class in Europe, and established a new school of foreign as well as of domestic fiction. The novel and the monthly magazine emerged during the same generation. Together with the polite essay, they helped to abolish pedantry, and we may justly say that they brought the development of modern English prose literature to a degree of finished grace and elegance not hitherto reached even in the noble examples furnished by Bacon, Taylor, Milton, and Sir Thomas Browne, who wrote as men must write who have not been brought into intimate accord with the idiomatic expression of a general audience.

# CHAPTER II

## THE DIDACTIC ERA

POPE'S succession to Dryden, who made such a point of "wit-writing," was lineal and natural. He was a boy of twelve when Dryden died, but before that, while studying with a priest in London, since his religious faith debarred him from the school privileges of Protestant youth, he had sometimes crept into Will's Coffee-House to get a glimpse of the older poet, who was also much the greater poet —especially in his later career, after he had turned from his French models to Shakespeare and to Nature for his inspiration. The pupil so far outdid the master in wit-writing as to leave behind and out of sight every natural emotion. The secret of his domination of the first half of the eighteenth century was his superficial didacticism, exquisitely adapted to a polished age, poignantly satirical, but as deftly disposed as the turns of a lady's fan or the steps of a minuet.

Johnson's didacticism, which gave him an equal dominion over the second half of the century, was of another sort—distinctly original as well as more serious and sincere. The ore of Shaftesbury's philosophy was necessary to Pope's shining coins of wisdom, but Johnson borrowed from nobody, at least from no contemporary, while others—even so eminent a man as Joshua Reynolds—were his confessed debtors. He made concessions to the age; courtliness was not difficult to him—he put on a scarlet coat when attending the performance of his tragedy; and pomp was only too easy. He was deeply religious, but no Pharisee, as is shown by his tolerance of mirth-making and by his friendships with Savage and Beauclerc. He had a large heart, as expansive as his vocabulary; large graciousness, if few graces; was a lover of ceremony, and doubtless never interrupted the "exercises of the fan." Still, we wonder how in the literary circles of the metropolis he secured and retained to the end of his life the undisputed position of dictator. Certainly very important concessions must have been made by the age to him; and quite as certainly these imply a considerable, if not radical, change in the mind, if not in the heart, of polite London.

The demand for didacticism is what mainly fixes our attention in this whole eighteenth-century comedy, in which contradictory elements are so strangely commingled. In the history of the preceding century our wonder has not ceased that the Commonwealth could have been established before we are equally surprised to see it so easily and utterly

abolished. But that which made the Commonwealth possible—something which appears recur-
rently in the whole woof of English history, and
which is deeper than Puritanism or Non-conformism—still remained the leaven of the public
thought, working beneath every compromise framed
for peaceful settlement. If we define this tenacious
element in political terms, as most often its repre-
sentatives were wont to define it, forthwith it is
seen to be first of all religious. The ghosts of Knox
and Cromwell and Bunyan and Milton would have
risen out of the dust of any great conflict in the
centuries after them, and to every generation after
them came the "Serious Call," which had its first
utterance ages ago in the voice of John the Baptist.

But in the eighteenth century there was no dust-
raising conflict; one blast from any really prophetic
trumpet would have crumbled the whole dainty
and fantastic fabric. Deism was fashionable, and
in such a society the conventional moralist was in
demand; and in the middle of the century the town
wanted a more positive didactician than Pope had
been. This they got in Johnson—a violently weak
preceptor. Literature at the same time gained in
him a violently weak critic. He swept everything
before him without smashing any precious traditional furniture. He suited all classes. No Non-
conformist could complain of a man who opened his
most important literary undertakings with prayer,
and who had no hesitation in branding the scepti-

cal Bolingbroke as a "scoundrel"; and his persistent Toryism endeared him to courtiers and conservatives. In the assemblies of the "Blue-stockings" he reigned supreme.

Johnson's most characteristic essays were published in the *Rambler*, which he started in 1750 and concluded in 1752. It was published twice a week, and all but four or five of the numbers were written by Johnson. Samuel Richardson, the novelist, was one of the outside contributors; the others were women. The collection of these essays in six volumes passed through twelve editions in London alone, and was considered by the author's admirers superior to anything in periodical literature, the more judicious of them with evident reluctance excepting some numbers of the *Spectator!* Johnson himself, more generous as well as juster, said: "Whoever wishes to attain an English style, familiar but not coarse, and elegant but not ostentatious, must give his days and nights to the volumes of Addison."

The industrious Doctor was at the same time engaged upon his English Dictionary, the exactions of which led to the abrupt termination of the *Rambler*, but he found time for occasional contributions in the same didactic vein to the *Adventurer*, established by his friend and imitator, Dr. John Hawkesworth, assisted by Richard Bathurst, a physician whom Johnson most dearly loved, and Dr. Joseph

Warton. The essays in the *Rambler*, and the Dictionary, which was completed in 1755, fully established Johnson's reputation. As preceptor and critic he met the exacting but superficial and limited needs of his own time, though he met those of no later generation. He had no profound comprehension of life or of literature, but within his limitations his logical analysis was accurate and his apprehension quick and vivid. Without charm, sententious beyond any other writer, he had a grave felicity of expression. He and the versatile Garrick, the vagabond Goldsmith, and the polite Chesterfield were characteristic types, any one of which would have made the fortunes of a novel. As depicted in Boswell's pages, they are more interesting than the persons in any society fiction of Fielding or Richardson. His levees, in which, from two o'clock in the afternoon—in his later years his usual hour of rising—until four, he was in the habit of receiving his intimate acquaintances and such unknown scribblers as chose to call upon him, would have furnished Smollett with material, of another kind, but as interesting as that obtained from association with his companions of the Fleet. But, while in many ways appealing to humorous sensibility, Johnson was not a successful humorist even in his more leisurely days when, in 1758, he started the *Idler*, having in view essays in a lighter vein. He was assisted in this undertaking by contributions from Sir Joshua Reynolds and Bennet Langton.

Johnson had thought of devoting his riper years to a periodical which should be called the *Bibliothèque*, and be mainly a review of contemporary Continental literature. The project was abandoned, but it is interesting as a reversion to the earliest type of the English literary periodical toward the end of the seventeenth century — literary in the bibliographical sense and intended only for the learned. About the middle of the eighteenth century this type had come to have a popular development. The *Museum* was a literary magazine as well as a review. The *Monthly Review*, started by Ralph Griffiths in 1749, was the first to assume the distinctly modern style of such publications, and endured for nearly a century. It represented Whiggism and Non-conformism. The Tory and Church interest established its rival, the *Critical Review*, which was edited by Smollett, the novelist, supported by Johnson, and by Robertson, the historian. Toward the end of the century these reviews increased in number, and, whatever partisan or religious interests they stood for, were always the dependencies of their publishers, tenders to their business. The first critical periodical of a high order, independent of the publisher, was the *Edinburgh Review*, established in 1802 by Sydney Smith, Jeffrey, Scott, and Brougham. Scott, seven years later, persuaded John Murray to establish its rival Tory competitor, the London *Quarterly Review*.

Returning to the preceding half-century, we find Dr. Johnson as closely associated with the *Literary Magazine* during the two years before he started the *Idler* as he had been at the beginning of his career with the *Gentleman's Magazine*. His learned contributions to this new periodical, which had more affiliation with the review than with the popular monthly, were better suited to his attainments than would have been the work calculated to give distinction to his projected *Bibliothèque*. After his *Rasselas*, written in 1759, he did no important original work. His pension of three hundred pounds, granted the next year by the new king, George III., reduced him to his native indolence, and thereafter he was known mainly by his conversation, which was more brilliant than his writing and showed a better art.

During Johnson's life, which ended in 1784, there was no popular monthly periodical of the type established by Cave in the *Gentleman's Magazine*, excepting its successful imitator and rival, the *London Magazine*. Each of these was greatly improved by the eager competition between them. Cave was driven to the verge of illustrated journalism, resorting to the novel attraction of engravings. The *Scots Magazine*, the first published in Scotland, is worthy of honorable mention, the length of its career, from 1739 to 1817—really to 1826, through its continuation as the *Edinburgh Magazine* — demonstrating its stable worth.

The essay periodical held its field through the entire century of which it was eminently characteristic. We have mentioned only a few periodicals of this class, but there were many others: the *Connoisseur*, to which the poet Cowper was a contributor; Fielding's *Champion* and *Covent Garden Journal;* the *World*—"written by gentlemen for gentlemen" —edited by Edward Moore, who had for his contributors such "gentlemen writers" as Chesterfield, Horace Walpole, and Soame Jenyns; the *Bee* and the *Citizen of the World*, by Oliver Goldsmith; the Edinburgh *Mirror* and its successor the *Lounger*, both of which were distinguished by the humorous contributions of Henry Mackenzie — besides scores of less important publications.

As we have seen, periodicals of this class were usually started and owned by individuals. This had been the case since Defoe issued his *Review*. Often a newspaper would be temporarily set up, as Wilkes's *North Briton* was, to plead some special cause, serving the same purpose as the old pamphlet. The publishing enterprise, as distinct from the trade of bookselling, was yet in its infancy, and the joint interest of author and publisher, now so commonly availed of, had not reached such a footing as would lead to its just appreciation by either party. What seems equally strange to us is that these essay periodicals, made thus dependent upon individual authorship, should have sought so sedulously to conceal the names of their authors. But the anonymity seems to have helped rather than hindered their success with the public, as was the case later with the Waverley Novels. It is significant that thus early in the history of periodical literature the thing written rather than the name of the writer gave assurance of worth.

The fiction of the time was but the reflection and expansion of the moral essay. Richardson was as didactic as Johnson, and even longer-winded. His epistolary fiction showed a softer sentiment than was germane to the period, and which degenerated into the mock-sentiment of Sterne. It was in both something quite different from the natural feeling shown in Addison's and Steele's essays—something, too, which, as exhibited in Richardson, was exasperating to Fielding, who deliberately set himself to the truthful portrayal of human nature, but whose realism was shallowly pessimistic. At the end of the century, the Irish tales of Maria Edgeworth presented living men and women, and, but for their obviously didactic purpose, might be regarded as anticipations of Jane Austen's novels in the very next decade—the first examples in fiction of a crisp and wholly natural realism. Hannah More was more of a religious preceptor than a novelist—but there were two of her: one the young woman who moved as a delighted listener in the circle of Johnson and Garrick, and who wrote plays; the other, the mature Hannah, who had come to believe that play-going itself was morally reprehensible, who wrote didactic poetry and tracts and stories that were sermons, and who, unlike Miss Edgeworth, believed in "conversion."

This persuasion of Hannah More's, that there is such a thing as a change of heart, and that it is something worthy of all effort to bring about in human-kind, leads us back to what we were saying about that leaven which in every age is working in English thought and feeling. The world of fashion is naturally ritualistic, and the leaven we refer to had little chance of effectively working beneath the formalism of eighteenth-century society, but it was working in a little circle at Oxford, before the middle of the century, as it had been for a long time among the unpolite multitude, preparing the way for preachers like Whitefield and John Wesley, though the latter had a native dread of non-conformity. With this religious movement we have nothing to do here, save as it was a radical reaction against the formal ethics of the polite world which constituted the framework of its literature, its histories, and its philosophy.

Since Milton there had been no development of the highest order of imaginative prose or poetry. The tides of human feeling were regulated by common sense, which eschewed romance and mysticism. Even fiction did not venture to transcend the facts and circumstances of the actual contemporary life. Some critics, like the Warton brothers, Joseph and Thomas, protested against the generally conceded supremacy of Pope as a poet, showed leanings toward Spenser, and were inclined to the spirit of mediævalism, as Horace Walpole was to its form. Thomson, Gray, Collins, Shenstone, Young, Beattie, and Goldsmith yielded to the charm of Nature. Burns, in his surprising lyrics, uttered a spontaneous and half-wild note of revolt against everything artificial and conventional. Then, through the elemental tempest of the French Revolution, we are launched into the nineteenth century—into the restless currents of a new spirit of life and literature.

We have seen how directly associated with periodical literature all the most characteristic writers —even the novelists—were in the eighteenth century. It is significant, therefore, that fiction was so wholly excluded from serial publications. The essay periodical was, of course, too limited in its compass to make room for the successive instalments of a novel. The magazines and reviews, while they sought to furnish entertainment to their readers, seem to have regarded fiction as too frivolous to blend harmoniously with their graver contents. The novels, perhaps, were too prolix—if we may judge from the length of *Sir Charles Grandison* —even to serve as feuilletons for the newspapers. We know of but one instance of a novel of this period published originally in serial form—that of Smollett's *Sir Lancelot Greaves*, which appeared in the *British Magazine* in 1760. The novelists, in their attempt to make their stories as matter of fact as possible, seem to have been conciliating an obstinate moral antagonism to fiction.

Scarcely any of the important poems of the century appeared in periodicals, notwithstanding the prizes offered by Cave. Perhaps the inferior quality of the poems thus published served as a deterrent to the better class of writers, who preferred the dignity of book publication. Gray, who had worked several years upon his Elegy, upon its completion (the knowledge of which was committed to Horace Walpole, who was too much of a gossip to keep the secret) was asked by an editor to contribute it to his magazine, but he refused, and hurried forward its publication in a sixpenny booklet, though afterward he allowed it to appear in three separate magazines.

The literature due to the revival of Romanticism belongs, in its full emergence, to the nineteenth century, but it was foreshadowed in much of the best poetry of the eighteenth. In prose — especially in fiction—the line between the two centuries is quite sharply defined. It is a long stride from Walpole to Scott, from Mrs. Radcliffe's *Mysteries of Udolpho* to the novels of Jane Austen.

# CHAPTER III

HORACE WALPOLE, frivolous as he was, showed more insight than most of his contemporaries, when, some time after his sagacious prevision of the French Revolution, he said that the next century "will probably exhibit a very new era, which the close of this has been, and is, preparing." In every sphere of human activity the opening years of the new century bravely responded to his prophecy. In literature the transformation was a wonderful surprise, a genuine renascence, so that one looking back could not discern the elements out of which the new time had been fashioned. Only in Burns was there a prelusive suggestion of the possibility disclosed in Byron.

Scott and Byron occupied the foreground of the opening drama in the first quarter of the century; and upon these two figures the mental gaze of the world was concentrated, with an interest more significant than that which had attended the sensational career of Napoleon. These writers—one the great Unknown, the other only too well defined to the imagination of readers in every trait of his peculiar individuality—had an overwhelming appreciation and adulation from their contemporaries such as no future generation could give them. But there were others, like Coleridge, De Quincey, Lamb, Hazlitt, and that group of immortal poets, Wordsworth, Shelley, and Keats, not fully recognized in their own time, but, in our view, its crowning glory. The entire literature of the preceding hundred and fifty years is dwarfed by comparison with this one little period, thronged with genius.

During the first half of the century literary criticism and political discussion were the predominant elements in periodical literature, to almost the entire exclusion of fiction. Poetry, however, was likely to be found even in periodicals devoted to special objects, like the *Philosophical Magazine*, in which the verses were at the end of the number and conveniently detachable by those who had no taste for that kind of reading. It was through the pages thus contemptuously torn out and cast aside by his father that Crabbe was first inclined toward poetic composition. Dr. Mark Akenside, author of *Pleasures of the Imagination*, began his poetic career by contributions to the *Gentleman's Magazine*. Hazlitt, writing of Wordsworth's "Excursion" in the *Examiner*, pronounced its finest passages "little inferior to those of his classic predecessor, Akenside!"

# ENGLISH PERIODICAL LITERATURE

It was because of the special interest in politics and criticism that the *Edinburgh Review* secured early, and long maintained, its pre-eminence over the most entertaining of monthly miscellanies. It began almost with the century, and was for many years more characteristic of the new era than any other periodical. Even with the support of Scott, its rival, Murray's *Quarterly Review*, under the editorship of Gifford, never attained the literary distinction which Sydney Smith and, after him, Jeffrey gave to the *Edinburgh Review*.

Among the monthlies in the first quarter of the nineteenth century, the *London Magazine*[1] was singularly fortunate in its contributors. It was there that first appeared De Quincey's "Confessions of an English Opium-Eater" and Lamb's "Elia" essays. Thomas Hood was closely associated with this periodical before he established one in his own name, in which he published his "Song of the Shirt" and "The Bridge of Sighs." Among other writers for the *London Magazine* were Cunningham, Talfourd, Procter, Hartley Coleridge, and the peasant-poet Clare.

Colburn had started his *New Monthly Magazine* in 1814. The poet Campbell was its first editor, followed by Theodore Hook, Bulwer Lytton, and Ainsworth. Campbell later edited the *Metropolitan*,

[1] Quite a different affair from the magazine of the same name which had been started nearly a century earlier as a rival to the *Gentleman's Magazine*.

and was succeeded by Captain Marryat, many of whose sea tales appeared in that magazine.

One of the most interesting of periodical adventures in the first quarter of the century was the establishment of the *Liberal*—a literary journal planned by Lord Byron in Italy conjointly with Shelley and Leigh Hunt, who were then with him there, but to be published in London, with Hunt as editor. The consultation took place at Leghorn, a week before Shelley was drowned in the Gulf of Spezia. The *Liberal* was started in the summer of 1822, but only four numbers were issued, the first of these opening with Byron's famous satire, "The Vision of Judgment," two years before the poet's death. Leigh Hunt had ten years earlier set out on his journalistic career in the *Examiner*, established by his brother, in which appeared some of his most noteworthy sonnets. His most important writing was in the *Indicator*, in the *Companion*, and in the *Talker* —"A Daily Journal of Literature and the Stage," lasting during two years, and written almost entirely by himself.

These journals with which Leigh Hunt was associated—especially the *Examiner*, to which William Hazlitt was also a regular contributor—were the natural precursors of the justly celebrated London weekly papers devoted mainly to political comment and literary criticism, beginning in 1828 with the *Athenæum* and *Spectator*. The *Saturday Review*,

started in 1855, was the culmination of this order of
journalism, and suggests at once the names of such
writers as Edward A. Freeman, Goldwin Smith,
and Lord Salisbury. The first editors of the *Athenæum* were John Sterling and Frederick Denison
Maurice. Dr. Theodore Watts Dunton was for
twenty-five years the leading literary critic of this
journal, to which also he contributed many of his
most characteristic poems.

Returning to monthly periodicals, the establishment of *Blackwood's Magazine*, in 1817, by William Blackwood, the founder of the celebrated publishing house in Edinburgh, is the most notable
event in the history of English periodical literature.
It marked also the beginning of Edinburgh's brief
period of literary supremacy. Constable had become the object of envy, having secured the greatest prize in the literary market, the publication of
the Waverley Novels. He was the publisher of the
*Scots Magazine*, a respectable monthly which held
the field in the absence of any formidable competitor, also of the great Whig periodical, the plucky
and enterprising *Edinburgh Review ;* and just then
the Whigs were having everything their own way.
Blackwood's first attempt, in the *Edinburgh Monthly
Magazine*, confided to the charge of two faithless
and incompetent editors, proved a conspicuous failure, as mortifying to the publisher as it must have
seemed ridiculous to his great rival.

At this juncture two young men fresh from Oxford—John Wilson and J. G. Lockhart—attracted the notice of Mr. Blackwood, who enlisted their interest in his new enterprise. So, with these giddy but zealous and resourceful youths to drive the horses of the sun, the seventh number of the monthly appeared under the new name of *Blackwood's Magazine*. It was an amazing number for its brilliance, its rollicking fun, and its folly. It had in it occasion for several possible libel suits. The celebrated "Chaldee Manuscript" was the *pièce de résistance*—a satire, couched in Biblical language (probably at the suggestion of James Hogg, the "Ettrick Shepherd," who was admitted to the council of conspirators), directed chiefly against the former editors of the magazine, against the "crafty" Constable, and even against Scott. But it established the fame of *Blackwood*. There were other things in the number less worthy of its jolly concocters—an article contemptuous of Coleridge, and a foolish assault upon Leigh Hunt, under the caption of "The Cockney School of Poetry." The readers were promised a further consideration of this "Cockney School" criticising the *lesser* poets, Shelley and Keats! The effect intended had been accomplished. The magazine had made a tremendous sensation. The world of Edinburgh, and much of the world outside, had been upset. There was no such volcanic eruption afterward, though the hot lava continued to run afterward in the brilliant series of the "Noctes

Ambrosianæ," which was extended through seventy-one numbers.

The note had been given—a note as impossible to London as it was native to Edinburgh. Thenceforth it was understood that *Blackwood* might be anything else, but it could not be dull. Wilson, who was soon installed in the chair of Moral Philosophy in the University of Edinburgh, continued faithful to two generations of Blackwoods, but in each of these generations it was the publisher who was editor. Lockhart's contributions, if less buoyant, were of more substantial value during his ten years' service before he succeeded Gifford as editor of the *London Quarterly.* These were all young men, including the publisher, who had just turned forty; and the erratic young Irish genius, Dr. Maginn, heartily joined in their frolicsome adventure. One is reminded of that other group of young men who, fifteen years earlier, had with like enthusiasm started the *Edinburgh Review,* unrestrained by the natural prudence of a responsible publisher.

No other British monthly publication can show an array of contributors to match *Blackwood's* retrospect. In its early years it had the best of De Quincey, except his "Opium-Eater," but including his most sustained work, "The Cæsars," also his "Flight of a Tartar Tribe." Scott contributed to the first number an interesting brochure on "The Depravity of Animals." In 1821 Coleridge was a contributor. At a later period we find in its pages

33

Aytoun's "Lays of the Cavaliers" and such humorous prose tales as "The Glenmutchkin Railway"; Samuel Warren's "Diary of a Late Physician" and "Ten Thousand a Year"; political papers by Sir Archibald Alison; Michael Scott's "Tom Kringle's Lay" and "The Cruise of the *Midge*"; novels by Bulwer; Charles Lever's "Cornelius O'Dowd" sketches and "Tony Butler"; Mrs. Browning's "Cry of the Children"; and poems by Mrs. Hemans. George Eliot's "Scenes of Clerical Life" first appeared in *Blackwood*. Mrs. Oliphant's first story in the magazine, "Katie Stewart," appeared in 1852, and she received the proofs of it on her wedding-day. Among other contributors were Walter Savage Landor, Laurence Oliphant, and A. W. Kinglake.

One of the most thoughtful writers for *Blackwood* from 1839 to his death, in 1872, was William Smith, the author of the two greatest philosophical novels in the English language—*Thorndale* and *Gravenhurst*. In an article upon him, October, 1872, in the magazine which had published one hundred and twenty of his contributions, mostly literary reviews, with occasional tales and sketches of continental travel, the writer says: "No better type could be found of the true man of letters, the student, scholar, and civic. . . . That charm of culture which, next to genius, is almost the most delightful of mental conditions, was his in an eminent degree." When the *Athenæum* was started on its new career in

1828, under the editorship of John Sterling and F. D. Maurice, William Smith, then twenty years of age, wrote for it a series of eight papers signed "A Wool-Gatherer." The first of these papers was a plea for periodical literature. In 1842 he published his great play "Athelwold," which Macready put on the stage, himself taking the part of Athelwold, and Miss Helen Faucit that of Elfrida. Mr. Smith was the first choice of Professor Wilson as his successor in the chair of Moral Philosophy at Edinburgh University.

Between 1864 and 1890 William Wetmore Story, the American sculptor, whose poems and essays as much entitle him to remembrance as his statues, and whose writings in the *Atlantic Monthly* had won for him a select recognition, was a frequent and esteemed contributor to *Blackwood's Magazine*.

It is interesting to note that the success of *Harper's Magazine* in articles of travel, brought to Blackwood's attention by Sir Richard Burton, led him to write to William Smith, suggesting that he edit a Cyclopædia of Travel, to be published in monthly parts. From the fifties *Harper's* was in correspondence with the same eminent novelists who were contributing to *Blackwood*—Bulwer, George Eliot, Trollope, Blackmore, and Mrs. Oliphant. Thackeray never published in *Blackwood*. He offered to it some of his earlier work, which was declined; but he was always on friendly terms with the house.

Samuel Lover, the author of *Handy Andy*, was an early contributor to the *Dublin University Maga-*

*zine,* started in 1833. Several of Ainsworth's novels, illustrated by Cruikshank, were first published in *Bentley's Miscellany.* During the last half of the century every important writer of fiction has contributed his, or her, best work to periodicals, for serial publication or in the form of short stories. Some of the greatest of these have been editors as well as contributors.

Dickens's editorial connection with *All the Year Round* and *Household Words* is very well known. His first short fiction sketches had appeared in monthly magazines—the first of all, "A Dinner at Poplar Walk," in the *Monthly Magazine* (not the *New Monthly*) in December, 1833. "Horatia Sparkins" was published in the *New Monthly,* February, 1834; "The Bloomsbury Christening" in the same, April, 1834, and "The Boarding-House," in the following number. It was to this last that the name of "Boz" was first signed. The earlier sketches were anonymous. Thackeray wrote for *Fraser's,* and was for some time the editor of *Cornhill.* Afterward, under the editorship of Sir Leslie Stephen, Henry James, Louis Stevenson, and Thomas Hardy were contributors to *Cornhill.* George Meredith, for a considerable period associated with the publishing house of Chapman & Hall as its literary adviser, came into close relations with young writers of fiction. It was by his advice that the first novel written by Thomas Hardy was not published. He was editor of the *Fortnightly Review*—in the establishment of which Anthony Trollope took an active part—during John Morley's absence in America. Several of his novels were first published in that periodical. His "Adventures of Harry Richmond" appeared first in *Cornhill*.

It is interesting to know—as we do from a letter of Robert Browning to the Storys, March 19, 1862, first published in Henry James's *William Wetmore Story*—that Browning, who had contributed several poems to *Cornhill*, was offered the editorship of that magazine to succeed Thackeray.

The great English essayists, from Sydney Smith to Charles Whibley, have been contributors to periodicals—for the most part to leading reviews.

Carlyle's first writings were published in the *Edinburgh Cyclopædia*, then edited by Brewster. Some of his early work appeared in *Fraser's*. His "Life of Schiller" was published in the *London Magazine*. He wrote for the *Edinburgh Review* his remarkable papers on German literature. His "Sartor Resartus" was published in *Fraser's*, and was received, we are told, "with unqualified dissatisfaction." George Eliot was in 1852 assistant editor of the *Westminster Review*. James Anthony Froude was for fourteen years the editor of *Fraser's*. William Allingham, the poet, was associated with him as assistant editor in 1870, and succeeded him in 1874. David Masson, the biographer of Milton, was the first editor of *Macmillan's Magazine*, in the early numbers of which Thomas Hughes's "Tom

Brown at Oxford" appeared serially. In the same magazine were published Tennyson's "Lucretius," Charles Kingsley's "Water Babies," Carlyle's "Shooting Niagara and After," Pater's "Gaston de Latour," Sir George Trevelyan's "The Competition Wallah," George Eliot's "The Breakfast Party," and Kipling's "The Incarnation of Krishna Mulvaney." Among other contributors in the course of its career, which closed in 1907, were Matthew Arnold, Gladstone, Anthony Trollope, Stevenson, Mark Pattison, Sir Walter Besant, Leslie Stephen, and Cardinal Manning.

Walter Pater contributed to the *Westminster* and largely to the *Fortnightly Review*. One of his Imaginary Portraits, "Apollo of Picardy," appeared first in *Harper's Magazine*.

Matthew Arnold's "Literature and Dogma" was published in *Cornhill*. Richard Jeffries, first a journalist on a local paper, was afterward, in the early seventies, a contributor to *Fraser's*.

The names of the writers we have mentioned, and the titles of the periodicals, are suggestive of the spirit which, after the cold crystallization of the two preceding centuries, created and organized a new order of imaginative literature in poetry, fiction, and criticism. This literature may not display the buoyancy and freshness of imagination which characterized the greatest Elizabethan literature, with which alone it may be compared, but it has developed a wholly new interpretation of life, faith, literature, and art, as well as of Nature.

# CHAPTER IV

## EMINENT AUTHORS IN JOURNALISM

THE intimate association of eminent writers of the nineteenth century with periodicals is, in a general way, recognized by intelligent readers. But if we attempt to trace this connection by directing to it something more than casual attention, certain features of it are disclosed which are interesting in themselves as well as in their relation to memorable writers.

The history of the daily newspaper, if anything so evanescent and at the same time so complex as this species of journalism could be caught and held within the meshes of the historian's net, would present many striking disclosures. Fielding and the greatest writers of his day were influential journalists. The Letters of "Junius" were published in the *Public Advertiser*. The London *Morning Post* at the beginning of the nineteenth century was especially favored by the contributions of important writers. Coleridge wrote for it, also Southey and Arthur Young; and it was the repository of Mackworth Praed's society verses, Tom Moore's lyrics, and some of the best of Wordsworth's sonnets. There, in 1800, appeared Coleridge's "Character of Pitt." Charles James Fox attributed the rupture of the hastily patched-up treaty of Amiens to Coleridge's essays in that paper.

James Montgomery, the poet, was the editor of a provincial newspaper. De Quincey, before he became known through his more characteristic writings, was for a year the editor of the *Westmoreland Gazette* in Kendal. George Meredith began his literary career as an editor of an eastern counties newspaper. He was afterward the special correspondent of the *Morning Post* during the Austro-Italian war of 1866. In the early forties Dickens was on the staff of the *Morning Chronicle*, in which paper, a generation earlier, Hazlitt had done his most important political work. Southey was at one time offered the editorship of the London *Times*. The same position was offered to Tom Moore for a year, during the illness of Barnes, who was at the time editor of that journal. Laurence Oliphant and Richard Monckton Milnes were its regular correspondents in the fifties. Thackeray was for some time its literary critic. The famous Irish journalist and poet, Francis O'Mahoney, "Father Prout," was, in the late fifties, the Paris correspondent of the London *Globe*, in which his letters made a literary sensation. William Allingham reports in his "Diary" that the *Globe* is said to have ordered a font of Greek type to meet the emergency devolved upon it by Father Prout's copious quotations from the classics. Robert Hichens, before he became known as a novelist, was associated with the London *World*.

In America, as soon as there began to be a literature at all it was through weekly, monthly, and quarterly periodicals that it found its way to the public rather than through the daily press, though some of Whittier's and Longfellow's earliest poems were published in newspapers, and Margaret Fuller was a regular contributor to the New York *Tribune*. The most distinguished American men of affairs or of letters, from Benjamin Franklin to Charles Dudley Warner, who have conducted or contributed to newspapers have done so mainly as publicists rather than as literary men. This is true of even the poet Bryant. Yet our principal dailies have always been enriched by picturesque sketches of travel, by humorous portrayals of character, by more or less able criticism, by contemporaneous poetry of varying degrees of excellence; and in recent years they have often published fiction contributed by the most popular writers of the time. Bayard Taylor and Mark Twain won their first laurels in the daily newspaper. Whittier was in his younger days editor of the *Essex Gazette*, in Haverhill, and William Gilmore Simms of the Charleston *City Gazette*, in South Carolina.

In England the position of the daily relatively to other periodicals, as to literary quality, has been very much the same that it has been in America.

Franklin had been moved by the success of the *Gentleman's Magazine* to start in Philadelphia the *General Magazine*, which ran through six months. We are not writing a history of periodical literature, and shall not attempt to trace the origin, growth, or extinction of the vast number of publications which have come into being since the establishment of the *North American Review*, which marks the beginning of American literature and has the unique distinction of numbering among its contributors nearly every great American writer, apart from its claim to the most distinguished succession of editors, among whom were such eminent men of letters as the elder R. H. Dana, Edward Everett, James Russell Lowell, and Charles Eliot Norton. It is significant that the first great imaginative poem written by an American, Bryant's "Thanatopsis," first appeared in the *Review* in 1817, followed a year later by the same writer's characteristic lyric "To a Water - fowl." Dana's equally remarkable poem, "The Buccaneer," was not published till 1827.

Longfellow's articles on the Romance Languages were published in the *North American Review*. William H. Prescott contributed to the *Review* two elaborate articles on Italian poetry in 1828 and 1831. The second of these was first accepted by Lockhart for the *London Quarterly*, but the publication was so long delayed that Prescott reclaimed the manuscript. He contributed to the *North American* an article on Molière in 1828 and, in 1849, a review of

Ticknor's *Spanish Literature*. Of his reviews and fugitive contributions to literary magazines he seems to have had a contempt like that which Lockhart showed for his own work of that sort. "Ephemeral trash," he called it, which "had better be forgotten by me as soon as possible." But he allowed Bentley, his London publisher, in 1845, to issue this material in a volume entitled *Critical and Historical Essays*, which the Harpers at the same time published in America.

Bryant as early as 1818 contributed to the *North American Review* an article on American poetry. We get some idea of the poverty of his theme from the names of the poets commemorated by him in his article—the Reverend John Adams, Joseph Green, Francis Hopinkson, Doctor Church, Philip Freneau, Trumbull, Dwight, Barlow, Humphreys, Hopkins, and William Clifton.

American men of letters at that time devoted their attention more to periodicals than to the writing of books. Philadelphia in the twenties and thirties, though she had no great individual author like Bryant or Cooper or Irving, could justly claim pre-eminence as the great literary magazine centre. Even as late as 1843 Hawthorne, Whittier, and Lowell seem to have been attracted to that centre. *Graham's Magazine* was then the most popular miscellany in America. Longfellow's "Spanish Student" first appeared in the pages of this periodical in 1842.

The first important literary periodical published in New York was the *Atlantic Magazine* (1824), which soon became the New York *Monthly Review*, of which R. S. Sands and William C. Bryant were the chief supporters. Bryant had, in 1824, come to New York, prompted by the advice of Henry Sedgwick (a brother of the poet Catharine M. Sedgwick), a prominent lawyer in that city. Here he met Cooper and Halleck, also Jared Sparks, who had just assumed the editorship of the *North American Review*. Returning to Great Barrington, he contributed poems to the *United States Literary Gazette*. In 1825 he came back to New York and, with Henry J. Anderson, undertook the editorship of the New York *Review*. His "Death of the Flowers" was published in that periodical—also Halleck's "Marco Bozzaris." Bryant began his work on the New York *Evening Post* in 1827, two years later becoming editor-in-chief. Before coming to New York, Bryant, like Hawthorne, had found favor with "Peter Parley," the pseudonym of S. G. Goodrich, the Hartford publisher, who issued an annual, called the *Token*, and in many ways gave encouragement to young New England authors.

Poe's "Raven" was first published in the New York *Mirror* in 1845. This publication was, by permission, in advance of the regular issue of the poem in the *American Whig Review*, to which it was originally contributed. Poe was for a time editor of the *Southern Literary Messenger*, and then of the

*Gentleman's Magazine*—afterward *Graham's*. Later he was associated with Charles F. Briggs on the *Broadway Journal*.

In the early thirties Oliver Wendell Holmes contributed to the *New England Magazine* two papers under the caption of "The Autocrat of the Breakfast-Table." Thus it happened that when in 1857 he resumed the series in the *Atlantic Monthly*, he did so with the connective remark: "I was just going to say."

N. P. Willis, the most picturesque figure in antewar periodical literature, was in 1829 editor of "Peter Parley's" *Token* and, about the same time, of the *Mirror*, having among its contributors Hawthorne, Motley, Hildreth, Albert Pike, and Park Benjamin. His most striking venture in this line was the establishment, in 1839, of the New York *Corsair:* "A Gazette of Literature, Art, Dramatic Criticism, Fashion, and Novelty." Thackeray wrote for it letters from London, Paris, Peking, and St. Petersburg, which afterward made up his *Paris Sketch-Book*. In his later years Willis was closely associated with the *Home Journal*, to which Thomas Bailey Aldrich was a contributor.

In 1843 James Russell Lowell started a magazine called the *Pioneer*, which ran for only three months, but numbered among its contributors Hawthorne, Poe, Whittier, and Elizabeth Barrett, afterward Mrs. Browning. At about the same time Emerson, Margaret Fuller, and George Ripley were conducting the *Dial*, which, though not the organ of the Transcendentalists at Brook Farm, expressed the views and sentiments of that community.

Charles Fenno Hoffman, the novelist and poet, was the first editor of the *Knickerbocker Magazine*, which had been established in New York in 1833. Hawthorne, Irving, and nearly every important writer of the country contributed to this entertaining magazine during the first twenty years of its existence. Longfellow's "Psalm of Life" first appeared in this magazine, anonymously. J. G. Whittier reprinted it in his newspaper, and said that the nine verses were "worth more than all the dreams of Shelley and Keats and Wordsworth."

Walt Whitman, seventeen years before he became famous as the author of "Leaves of Grass," was the printer, editor, and publisher of a weekly newspaper in Huntington, Long Island. He had before this undertaking contributed to newspapers and magazines. His weekly newspaper, the *Long Islander*, was abandoned by him after two years' experience in 1840. The next year he gained his first literary success in the *Democratic Review* with a poem entitled "Death in a School-Room." Other contributions to this periodical were signed Walter Whitman. He was a contributor to the *Mirror*, wrote verses for the *New World*, on which he was a compositor, and was successively the editor of the *Aurora* and the *Tatler*. In 1846–47 he was the editor of the *Brooklyn Eagle*. It was in some antislavery poems in the New York *Tribune* that he first adopted irregular metrical forms.

It was in the last half of the century that the American magazine for the first time ceased to be a miscellany and became a thoroughly well-organized complement of a for the first time well-organized American literature. The national expansion westward, especially after the acquisition of the Pacific coast, had developed a literary need which magazines like *Graham's* and the *Knickerbocker* could not meet; and it was in the natural course of things that the publishing house which, in its book publications, was most intimately associated with this continental growth, in the line of already developed or newly awakened intellectual tastes and demands, should establish a magazine like *Harper's*. It was equally inevitable, because of the existence of a group of remarkable writers like Lowell, Longfellow, Hawthorne, Holmes, Whittier, Emerson, and Thoreau, all living in the vicinity of Boston, that the New England movement of that time should find its expression in the *Atlantic Monthly*. These two were the original types, repeated, with important variations, in the other great magazines which have since been established. With scarcely an exception every distinguished writer of books during this period has been also a contributor to magazines.

Periodical literature has done more for the American people than for any other. It had a considerable development before there was an American literature, meeting the intellectual needs of a sturdy race which, while its energies were engaged in the solution of difficult practical problems rather than in the writing of books, was yet intelligent and keenly curious. After that period, which in eighteenth-century America as well as in England was characterized by "common-sense," and of which Benjamin Franklin was the typical representative, had been broken up by the war for independence, the re-awakened thought found political rather than literary expression, yet in the new generation there were doubtless more readers of Scott and Byron than in the previous one there had been of Dr. Johnson, or, in the one before that, of Addison. While orators like Fisher Ames, John Randolph, and William Wirt were being developed instead of writers like Coleridge and Wordsworth, yet, even in the conservative *Portfolio*, extracts were given from the most recent English books and periodicals and from the new English poets. We may call it colonialism, a confession of dependence, but this eclecticism in periodical literature furnished a necessary complement of American culture, and the fact that it was demanded and eagerly accepted by readers shows that there existed the sensibility to imaginative literature, though the literary faculty was diverted to every other than its own distinctive field.

In the first year of the fifties, when *Harper's Magazine* began its career, there were no really great American writers of fiction. We had had our Cooper and Irving and, far in the retrospect, our Charles Brockden Brown. Poe had already finished his career in this field. But, in England, Scott and Ainsworth, Maria Edgeworth and Jane Austen, had been succeeded by Lever, Bulwer, Dickens, Thackeray, and George Eliot. Outside of our large cities, and especially in the new West, this great fiction was not readily accessible in book form, and a vast majority of the people were dependent upon a magazine which should undertake to meet its need by the publication serially, but in their entirety, of the best current novels of the day. The magazine which did effectively undertake this publication, through communications already established with English authors and publishers, was accomplishing an important work for American literature.

The short-story writers, who were to displace T. S. Arthur and the sentimental contributors to *Graham's Magazine* and other miscellanies of that order, were stimulated to do their best by reading the best, and the powers thus evoked produced work in this field of fiction which was not only original in structure and quality, but far surpassed all English models. Not less effective was the stimulation of artists through the use of illustrations, until the original work of Abbey and Reinhart and Pyle was as far above that of "Porte Crayon" as the short stories of Miss Wilkins and Owen Wister surpassed Fitz-James O'Brien's.

The intimate blending of a magazine with the

thought and life of a whole people, whose intellectual and emotional sensibility was so quickly responsive to its imaginative literature, and whose curiosity was so fully met by its articles of travel and exploration and by others of an informing character, making it for them a Real Encyclopædia of the living world, was never so fully realized as in the career of the periodical which was the first example of its type—that of a popular illustrated magazine. It had the exclusive advantage of this intimacy for fully twenty years before others of the same type and class entered the field, amicably sharing its popularity.

Equally illustrious, within its deliberately chosen limitations, has been that other type of magazine established by the *Atlantic Monthly* — a type consistently maintained for half a century, and of which it has been the single successful example. It began its career at the most propitious moment, when every individual member of the most distinguished galaxy of writers which this country has ever produced—even outrivalling in stability of literary character the celebrated Edinburgh group in the first quarter of the century—was at his best. It was edited from the beginning by such eminent men of letters as Lowell, Howells, Scudder, and Aldrich; and, after the brilliant constellation of writers who gave it its earliest distinction had vanished and the peculiar literary supremacy of Boston with it, the course of empire inevitably tending to New

York, the *Atlantic* still remained unrivalled in its own field.

Each of the two types which we have been considering is remarkable for its flexibility, which has been shown not only in such changes as occur in progressive development, but in such as are of an evolutionary character. The *Atlantic*, standing especially for the individual expression of its writers, was too catholic in its selection to depend entirely upon a single group of authors, and the passing of that most distinguished group was simultaneous with the emergence elsewhere, in a broader field, of writers worthy to take their place. So, in the other type, when, in the general progress of the country, the people ceased to depend upon the illustrated periodical for either elementary information or supplementary education, the field of imaginative literature in fiction and the short story and in the higher order of creative essay and sketch was enlarged and diversified as if by new species. Fresh disclosures in science and in history took the place of the elementary lesson.

The last half of the century may be called the age of Criticism, in the large sense of that term, as used by Matthew Arnold when he defined poetry as "the criticism of life." Fiction, in its higher function, is the critical interpretation of life; and it was when fiction came into its own that a fresh and mighty impulse was given to periodical literature, as a means

## CHAPTER VI

### THE AMERICAN AUDIENCE

IN the criticism of contemporary literature there has always been a tendency on the part of academically trained critics to disparage the present as compared with the past. This tendency discloses the vice as well as the virtue of that conservatism which has the long view backward but the limited view of the present and future, and which, while it holds to the established best, ignores the best that is in the making.

As a corrective, we need for literature such a plea as Professor Lounsbury is in the habit of interposing for language—a protest against the purist and an apology for legitimate freedom and flexibility. Professor Lounsbury's defence of new locutions should find, for a proper adjustment of our critical view, a counterpart in some equally effective justification of new literary styles.

Our judgment is not merely a matter of orientation—the turn of our thought backward through well-worn channels to familiar traits and canons which have the sanction of classical authority. We incur the peril of a vast ignorance if, in our regard for the continuity of human culture, we confine ourselves to a retrospective view, and disregard, or court only for our amusement, the novel phenomena which constantly present themselves in the field of literature. So a follower of the Hesiod cult might have regarded the invasion of the Homeric influence, which turned out to be the inspiration of what was best in Hellenic art and literature. So Dr. Johnson must have looked upon the swelling current of romanticism which swept away the artificial decorations and conventions of two generations of English classicism.

We of the East, accustomed from the beginning to look across the Atlantic for our models and inspirations, have given too little heed to the development of the new spirit in the West, excepting as it has been embodied in the personality of a statesman like Lincoln or of a humorist like Mark Twain. That way lies for us the freshly unveiled Pacific, our dream of Empire, and the magnificent realization of material grandeur and enterprise—a realm of adventure which for more than fifty years has been invested with the glamour of Argonautic romance. We have felt all this, but we have failed to comprehend the mental attitude of the people who have accomplished these material results—an attitude developed in the light and shadow, and under the stimulus and oppressiveness, of such achievement.

The strenuous men of the West are absorbed in schemes of mechanical progress and commercial expansion, while social and intellectual culture is to a great extent established and maintained by the women. It appears, too, that, as the men admire those intellectual functions which they have no time for, so the women take peculiar pride in the splendid material achievements of their husbands and brothers, and seek to rival these in the field so wholly committed to their charge — to do as striking things in society and literature as the men are doing in bridge-building, in sky-scraping architecture, in gigantic business combinations.

This was not the case thirty years ago on the Pacific coast, though it is so to-day. There and then it was from men that we heard the note of an original departure both in literature and art, and we had the reward of our listening. How distinct was the local color and flavor of the Pacific literature of that period! Now the conditions in California are much the same as in the Middle West, save that there is on the part of the predominant women greater tension of sensibility and mental activity.

What is now in evidence in this Western field is an immense and eager audience — eager for some things, and as firm in its protest against other things. What is its attitude? This, surely, is an interesting inquiry. The audience is the determining factor in the making of a literature; its demands are imperative. The West has been postulant from the beginning, and its present intellectual requirements have an importance in the shaping of our literature equal to that of its earlier economical demands in shaping the internal policy of our government.

What is the kind of literature that the West wants, and against what does this great audience forever utter its protest? The inquiry is the more pertinent because our new writers are called upon to choose between old and new methods of appeal. The question can never be whether the writer should abandon established standards of literary taste. No cultivated American audience, East, South, or West, advocates, much less demands, a lower literary art. Nor is the new writer's choice one between listening to the voice of England's Poet Laureate, Alfred Austin, on the one hand, calling him back to eighteenth-century ways, and, on the other, to the voice of Mrs. Atherton in her protest against what she calls a bourgeois literature.

Alfred Austin does not fairly represent the cause of fidelity to the continuity of culture; else he would not have with so easy agility, involving an implication of contempt, overleaped the entire and mightily vital Victorian era, to find, in Pope's time, the worthiest examples both of good writing and of an intellectual audience. Nor does Mrs. Atherton, in any fair sense voice the demand made by intelligent Western readers, or their protest. Her plea can hardly be said to adequately and exactly respond to the expectations of that Western culture which

has been developing during the last two generations
—expectations so just and reasonable as to be worthy
not only of the respect but of the careful consideration of all lovers of good literature.

Those of us who, during the period mentioned,
have given close attention to the course of books,
with reference to their appreciation in different sections of the country, remember that any literary
work of exceptional value, whether as a manifestation of genius or as a novel disclosure of spiritual
truth, whatever its reception elsewhere, has always
been sure of a hearty response from beyond the
Rockies, where was the nucleus of the early growth
of culture in the West. The people who migrated
from New England carried with them to their new
homes their intellectual tastes and habits, building
churches and schools and colleges, and establishing
newspapers; and while the South cherished local independence almost to the point of exclusiveness,
owing to its peculiar institution, the West long
cherished a feeling of dependence, beseeching means
of easy communication with Eastern centres, that
it might not be cut off from the currents of the old-
home and the Old-World culture. The demand of this
people, adventurous but unwillingly remote, for good
literature afforded an eager market for books; and
the one periodical that in those early days had a general circulation instinctively adapted itself to meet the
far-off need for such educational aliment as schools
and libraries could not furnish, while its fiction sup-

plied the wants of the imagination, and its illus-trated articles of travel brought the whole world to the mining-camp and the settler's cabin as well as to cultivated homes in comparatively isolated regions.

In the course of time has come the inevitable re-action; new currents of thought and feeling have been set in motion, arising from a new kind of civ-ilization which is not merely a reflection of the old, and whose peculiar traits indeed are more accent-uated now that it is in full communication with the world than in its earlier isolation. These pecu-liar traits are the result really of a slow and un-conscious development, and are intimate and sub-jective as distinguished from external peculiarities of tone, manner, and speech. They indicate modes of thought and feeling—the psychical attitude. If we were to express this attitude in positive terms, we should speak of it as vital, tense, and intuitively direct—just what we would expect of a culture which has come to follow the lead of feminine in-spiration. *Dux femina facti;* and this leadership, it must be admitted, is reinforced by the inspiration of all the great masters in the whole line of human culture. Very much of the energy engaged in this development is exhausted in social activities and for practical ends; it certainly does not as yet pro-duce many eminent authors, and the immediate atmosphere — the overpowering material environ-ment—is not conducive to great authorship, though by reaction the psychical sensibility is deepened, the result of which is an audience of distinguished readers whose attitude toward literature must have a profound influence in shaping and directing it.

We find it easier, therefore, to give an idea of the traits of this femininely conducted, though by no means effeminate, Western culture in somewhat negative terms. Open to all currents of the world's past and present thought and, as we have said, reinforced by them, it reacts upon them as it does upon its own immediate environment. As, in the latter case, the psychical rises to react upon the material, so against all the influences of the world's culture is developed an impatience of the traditional and conventional forms through which these influences offer their values. The values are appreciated, but the forms are repudiated—especially such old forms as seem the cerements rather than the fresh investiture of present and living thought.

This, in the main, is the protest, and it is a note more worth heeding than that of the Poet Laureate. Of course we are considering the demands made by a cultivated audience, which, while it lays little stress upon what Mrs. Meynell calls "the trick of education," does especially insist upon training, upon a thorough intellectual equipment as essential to authorship. In the West, as everywhere else, there is an outlying audience, clamoring for its own kind of satisfaction and getting it abundantly. The audience we have in view, though cultivated, is distinctly bourgeois and proudly calls itself middle-class; but it is the kind of middle-class which is produced by democracy in conditions which have freed it from the trammels of tradition and the masks of hypocrisy; it is non-conformist, not whiningly or fanatically, but instinctively, by an almost unconsciously developed attitude—an earnest psychical attitude which more intently regards the theme than any form of premeditated art in which the theme is expressed.

The feminization of culture is not exclusively a peculiarity of the West, or even of America; it is a characteristic of our period, of the stage which we have reached in our civilization. Democracy, too, has done its work in the East as well as in the West, though it has not destroyed so much wheat along with the tares. The fact that the leadership of Western culture is so exclusively feminine must in great measure account for its comparative sterility. Where this leadership is to a greater extent shared by both sexes and there is a considerable class of men not so absorbed in strenuous enterprise but that it has time to devote to art and literature, independently of social and practical considerations, there is more fruitfulness in the higher field of creative work.

Some characteristic Western traits of an earlier period have disappeared. In the present situation there is little chance for the development of humor or for the existence of the mood and temperament from which humor spontaneously flows. How much might as well as mirth—all the masterly traits, indeed, of the creative spirit—must in the nature of things vanish from a realm of culture so exclusively dominated by women! Equally true it is that, by just as natural limitations, many of the traits which we most highly prize as indispensable in our modern world—not merely of daintiness and grace but of spiritual strength—would be wanting under exclusive masculine domination.

But there is no sterility like that of a feminized culture, unruffled by the masculine spirit, vexed to its depths only by its own feverish unrest. There is in it no sense of the morning, of the springtime, no token of renascence. Mrs. Peattie confesses to this lack when she says: "If candor and splendor and truth are to come into American literature, they must come by way of immigrants from the nations of unabashed sentiment, who, singing songs in this land, sing with their faces turned to the sun—not toward a group of carping matrons sitting in conclave on all honest and free-spoken words."

It seems strange that a Western writer should indulge in this far-reaching orientation, looking to the effete Old World for the rejuvenescence of American literature.

We could not so effectively enter upon the consideration of the present conditions of American magazine literature as after repeating this cry from the

wilderness, having first led up to it and given a significance to its location by what we had to say about
what has long been and must continue to be the largest constituency of American books and periodicals,
about the importance of its demands in shaping the
course of our literature, about the value of its protest, and about its peculiar culture—its advantages
and its limitations.

But first we must let Mrs. Peattie's complaint
conclude itself, since it furnishes her explanation
of what is called "the deterioration of our literature."
"The matrons," she says, "have killed the New
England literature. They have edited the magazines, ruled the book publishers, and broken the
hearts of the poets. They will have an awful reck-
oning some day . . . when they shall stand and
tremble before the Truth, and find all their propri-
eties an insufficient barrier!"

Well, it would seem that the day of judgment has
already come, at least for magazine editors. For
Mrs. Peattie only repeats what the casual correspondents of newspapers and even newspaper editors have without end reiterated. If Mrs. Peattie
really meant to call magazine editors matrons—
that might seem original, and perhaps to some of
the group unpleasant, though, for ourselves, we
don't mind it; there is a kind of dignity in the title.
But the context forbids this idea of a personal in-
sinuation. She really refers to a very respectable

class of women for whom we shall interpose no defence—they need none. If they have done what Mrs. Peattie says they have done, their work seems to have been pretty effective, and we should leave them to their dreadful arraignment. In fact, however, they have done none of the things attributed to them. They have always been a very harmless, inoffensive kind of women, too busy with other things to edit magazines or to act as literary advisers to publishers. At least, in an experience of more than forty years in association with a publishing house, we have never known of any meddling on their part with the business, except in rare cases after the fact.

We have always understood that the publishers who issued *Jane Eyre* and *Adam Bede* did so without any previous consultation with matrons or any thought of them, leaving them to talk it over afterward with the same fearless freedom. We never knew a publisher to reject a novel that was on its literary and dramatic merits worth publishing, except when it was indecent or was likely to have an actually immoral influence—the kind of thing which would have been as unpleasant reading to himself as to any reader, even a matron. *Trilby* was published not only as a book but as a magazine serial. It was not immoral, though it was unmoral—as unmoral as childhood is. Two or three matrons wrote protesting letters, but most of the few complaints made came from men. Thomas Hardy's

*Tess of the D'Urbervilles* was published serially in *Harper's Bazar*, and his *Jude the Obscure* (under another title) in *Harper's Magazine*. If publishers of books and magazines err in this matter, it is likely to be on the side of daring, not from adventurous intention but in unconscious innocence. They are not afraid to confront Truth—even with a capital T.

Indeed, it is this very Truth, with all the candor and splendor that attend it and all its inherent majesty, that the best literature of to-day in books and magazines confronts without tremor. This is as true of our literature as of our science. It is a direct and intimate attitude, and we frankly credit the West with having helped us to it. But it is the trait of our time, as well in the East as in the West, however we may have come by it. It indicates a distinct advance in our culture, which in literature brings us ever more and more face to face with the truths of life, just as in science it insists upon the true representation of physical phenomena. The supreme interest of the greatest fiction of our time is in its psychical interpretations and disclosures. This interest excludes no really vital theme, but only that false and shallow and even meretricious masquerade of human passions and sentiments which vitiated the fiction of a former age, and which no cultivated reader now tolerates. Even Zola is pathologically true, and has his proper place in the respect of readers who seek that kind of truth. In

English and American fiction the writers who have developed the psychical method — among whom Henry James stands both as the type and as first in the exemplification of the type—have kept within the limits of a normal exposition. The good and evil are inseparably mingled in our human life— our chief wonder being, as Mrs. Deland has said, the badness of people who are called good and the goodness of those who are called bad—so that the shadows have their place in the brightest picture, and they are not to be evaded by any shuffling. We willingly follow where the path inevitably leads —to see life as it is.

We do not say that everything which could be published with propriety in a book could fitly be published in a magazine. The purchaser chooses his book; the magazine goes to an audience to which it is committed by a pledge, in part explicit, but for the most part a matter of implicit understanding. But the limitation does not arise from an embarrassing moral constraint. That is scarcely felt; the editor is not consciously aware of it; his resistance is against weak, unworthy stuff. There are doubtless authors who revel in brutalities, who enjoy an infernal habitation not for its purgatorial fires but for its sulphurous airs, and who complain because they may not make their descents before a polite audience; but these things do not come within the scope of the demand of any species of human culture.

# CHAPTER VII

EVERY magazine in the course of its development establishes an expectation as to the field it will occupy and the kind of themes it will treat. Hence arises its principal limitation. Fifty years ago, a popular magazine intended for general circulation must have been educational in a sense that it need not be to-day. For a long time it must have treated themes now wholly relegated to special periodicals. One thing it never could have excluded—that is, the best current literature.

It is fortunate in the interests of a general culture and of literature especially that a great magazine to-day may have as its distinguishing limitation the exclusion of specialties, retaining only within its scope such scientific, historical, and descriptive articles as are novel disclosures in their several fields. It may even avoid all timely or occasional topics, so adequately treated by the daily and weekly press, thus devoting nearly its entire space to what is known as the literature of power. The cultivated reader is so greatly the gainer by this that he will not complain, since whatever is omitted is easily accessible elsewhere, while he is not sure of having the best current literature, or of having so much of it, in any other way.

The contributor sometimes complains of the exclusion of some things in favor of others where the editor cannot say: "These lie outside the scope of our magazine." There is a law of selection by comparison. Out of a score of good things perhaps but one is chosen, the one considered the best in the editor's judgment, and yet the magazine is filled from month to month with these chosen contributions. Had the others been accepted also, they would never see the light except as excluding better things. It may be that among those rejected some one thing is ideally beautiful — a prose-poem, perhaps, which would be a delightful satisfaction to a few readers, to whom either by itself or together with other things having the same rare quality it should come in the shape of a book, to be read at leisure, and not, as in a magazine, mingled with elements out of harmony with it, not pitched to the same far-off note. This may be the case of a poem, an essay, or a story. This is simply saying that for magazine use the near, and still more the intimate, note is preferred. Of two poems having equal poetic merit—one concerning some object in nature, a bird or a flower, and the other a direct appeal of a human theme to human sensibility—the latter would be chosen. Yet a creation of the highest order, like Shelley's "Ode to the Skylark," would be choice - compelling. It is true even of books that the large polite audience—that upon whose patronage our best magazines depend— demands the intimate human appeal.

In our first-class magazines nature sketches find a place, in due proportion, and in greater variety than ever before. The charge against these magazines, that they have given up their space mainly to fiction and fail to meet the wants of readers in other directions, is made without due examination. New disclosures of physical phenomena; luminous interpretations of history; revisions of old and mistaken views based upon freshly discovered material; the most recent revelations of archæological exploration; the result of current sociological experimentation; studies of tendencies characteristic of the civilization of to-day and of imperfectly understood conditions of civilization in earlier times; studies also which are the result of travel and observation among peoples never before heard from and of the reaction of a creative imagination upon material which seemed familiar, but which for the first time yields to a new interpretation its inmost secrets, affording a fresh field of wonder; narrations of singular adventure—all this from writers the most authoritative, where first-hand authority is essential, and, as to those themes whose treatment depends for its interest upon genius, by writers acknowledged to be of the first rank, wholly apart from their contributions to magazines. In this summation of features we are not considering a magazine's contents taking a whole year into the view; a single number will contain something of nearly all this varied entertainment. The articles will not be elaborate, as in a review, but concisely comprehensive, suggestive, and illuminative; they are just what cultivated readers want.

There would not be so much fiction given in a magazine were it not true that in novels and short stories the life of this and other times has its most faithful portraiture, so that they stand for many an essay and article.

If we are all along confessing to certain limitations of the magazine, it is not unwillingly. We confess frankly that in literature the book and not the magazine is the supreme thing. In some ways the magazine conveys books to its readers, in serial fiction and in series of short stories and sketches and important articles—books which are among the best of their time. But, outside of fiction, the great books of all time stand by themselves in a world where the magazine is not. The exaltation of this world is in the matter of themes. So far as quality is concerned, the isolation does not exist. Though we have admitted that some things ideally beautiful, but appealing to a few select readers, are excluded from magazines, the exclusion is because of the remoteness of their themes, not because of their excellence. The magazines whose constituency is limited to a cultivated audience, one which is constantly increasing with the steady advance of culture, cannot meet the demands of that audience by the adoption of any standard lower than the best. It cannot seek writers whose sole aim is popularity or those who have achieved only that. It must have the best current literature obtainable, and therefore the most eminent writers of the time, and it gets these writers. The best current novels are published serially in magazines of this class. Who are the greatest writers of short stories and poems? It is these whose work is appearing in our magazines from month to month. Their first encouragement came from magazines. Liberal remuneration for their contributions has made it possible for many of them to persevere in literary work, and the work itself is better than that of any former period in the history of periodical literature. But, excellent as it is, the demand of the audience and therefore of the magazines is always for something better.

This is a sufficient answer to those who hold magazine editors responsible for "the deterioration of literature." The complaints made are contradictory, one to another. Some critics, who have given very little attention to the real character of magazine literature, assert that contributors in order to succeed must "write down" to it. The main complaint, in which many writers join, is that they are required to "write up" to it. This complaint has reference even more to themes that are excluded than to requirements as to style, though the one point usually implies the other. It is objected that the magazine editor "wants better bread than can be made of wheat," that he sets himself up as a "ruler of literature," trampling upon every spark of genius and repudiating all that is primal and elemental, and that he is especially shocked by the expression of "unabashed sentiment."

Everything in its place and time commands respect. Crudeness precedes development in all evolution. But it would be unjust to treat the complaint as a plea for crudeness. Much as it sometimes seems like it, it is not meant to be that. If we allow the complainant to state his own case, he would say that instead of favoring retrogression—a reversion to a lower order of development—he stands as the advocate of those reactions which especially characterize the most advanced stages of human civilization. The plant or the animal developed into new varieties by artificial selection, if again left to itself, reverts to its original type, and this might properly be called degeneration. But in human development the progress involves a series of reactions, peculiar to a rational consciousness, which is itself due to the breaking of vital currents, and which gains in stability with the increased complexity of the brokenness. All nature has this divided living, and the division is multiplication; but in man it has a peculiar significance because it is a psychical process, involving reflection which gives him the choosing will, so that in his progress he does not always go straight on in inevitable courses, but turns upon himself at will and, in spiral fashion, goes forward half of the time by going backward. Thus the call for the primal and elemental is forever recurrent, in each downward course of the spiral ascent.

This is all true and strictly philosophical. Man goes back upon himself in a way that Nature does not—except at vast intervals when she also declares: "I care for nothing, all shall go." This proclamation man — the most tropic of all beings — makes often in quick reactions and revolutions. His spirit builds for itself a complex edifice full of life and light in which for a time it rejoices; then it cherishes the edifice for itself, and as the surfaces harden it delights in giving them the polish they are ready to take; it refines all outward means of expression, revelling in forms of exquisite grace and measure, and multiplying the conceits and caprices of its architecture. Then the windows grow dull; there is death at the extremities where life has exhausted itself in accomplishments that now turn to vanities; the spirit, burdened by what seemed its weight of glory, is lulled to sleep by its muffled music. This is the course of every age, and at every fresh awakening of the human spirit the mortal coil of the formal structure is shuffled off, and in the rude light of the new morning, as in "the freshness of the early world," men are with the gods again, who are so poor that their gifts are only of raw material. What wonder that, when refinements become glosses and all our vesture a masquerade, we long for that primal poverty!

But the plea for the elemental in literature does not seem quite justified, since we already have had so much of it, the literary pendulum having so long swung that way. More than a century ago the reaction began against the perruque and pirouette in literary pantomime and all the artificialities of Queen Anne's time; it has been going on ever since, and it has gone so far that, by an opposite reaction, many look with a kind of envy to the formal graces of that remote period which have for them the fascination of the eighteenth-century minuet.

We in America have had our Walt Whitman, and if there is any variety of "unabashed sentiment" with which the fiction of the last twenty years has not made us acquainted, we are willing to forego further knowledge of it.

In good and bad literature—in that which appeals to the cultivated and that which panders to a lower taste—this reaction has done its best and worst for us. We do not mean to say that it has run its course, and that it has no new glories to disclose. Our attitude toward the mightiest realities of life, the most elemental truths, is more direct and intimate than ever before; and it is so in magazines as well as in books. The magazine editor has cherished rather than resisted it, and he expects of it, if nothing better than it has already yielded, yet a new revelation of its possibilities. It is true that he favors the most artistic—that is, the most developed—expression of intimate truths; for the characteristic trait of a period is sure not only to determine the writer's theme but to shape his style. Elemental truths may be conveyed more effectively in the exquisite art of Meredith, James, Hardy, Howells, Hewlett, and Mrs. Humphry Ward than in the uncouth forms which, because of their crudeness, may seem to some especially suited to their expression.

Nevertheless, the editors of our best magazines do not reject the contributions of the less developed writer who promises great things to come—great in rare art as well as in rare insight. Those writers now proclaimed the greatest were in their lesser day diligently fostered by these magazines.

The most unjust and, even on the part of those who ought to know better, the most prevalent complaint is that magazine editors suppress individuality, either by its entire exclusion or by its corruption through the imposed obligation to accommodate itself to editorial requirements. On the contrary, it is individuality that the wise editor most eagerly looks for and most sedulously cultivates. Apart from the wholly worthless stuff offered, more contributions are rejected because their writers have made a point of accommodation than for any other reason. It is only as a writer expresses himself, utters his own note, that he has any value. The most obviously "magazinish" thing is the most unmagazinable. Any attempt toward accommodation injures the contributor's chance of success.

There are limitations which the contributor does well to regard, but they are negative. Magazines intended for general circulation must, of course, exclude politics and theology. A magazine of this class must avoid the article too general in its treatment or too elaborate, also the article too special or too technical, assuming an audience devoted to a particular field; that is, it must not be distinctively an art, an historical, or even a literary magazine. Magazines differ, one from another, in their limitations. Some favor and some exclude the timely topic. But all must have variety, and this necessity imposes a limitation as to the length of individual contributions, though each of these, whether an article or a story, must have a scope adequate to the satisfaction of thoughtful readers, even at the sacrifice of variety.

As to quality, however, there is no limitation which excludes the highest excellence. As we have said, the book is the supreme thing; but not only does the magazine avail of this supreme value in its serial fiction, but in all its varied contents it demands, as to quality, the excellence which gives the best book its supremacy, and which so many books lack. A single number of a first-class magazine, though it fully serves the purpose for which it was created, and in its scope and quality gives satisfaction, may seem to the critic, though not a miscellany, still, at the best, a fragmentary collection; but taking the numbers *seriatim*, as the reader takes them, for a year, for a generation, they furnish a unique illustration of the progress of literature and, if illustrated, of art—a progress which the magazine has stimulated as well as exemplified.

The catholicity of magazines and their hospitality to young writers have done more than all other influences to build up our literature.

The audience is the determining factor in our literature. Whatever that is most creditable may be said of our best magazines reflects credit upon the culture of that audience, whose demands are not less exacting than its response is quick and generous. The whole country makes up this audience of to-day, and, whatever the diverse demands of different sections, these are equally worthy of respect and represent values which will be more evident for what they really are when distinct currents shall have fully reacted upon one another and blended into that harmony which shall characterize the American audience of the future.

## CHAPTER VIII

### THE PASSING OF ANONYMITY

IT is now so generally the custom of magazines to give the names of contributors that readers naturally find it difficult to understand why a contrary custom so long prevailed. If we were to show these readers the manifest virtues of anonymous authorship in periodical literature, they would then as naturally inquire why it has not been maintained. The time when *Harper's Magazine* began to give signed articles is within the memory of middle-aged readers, who will be surprised to learn that the step was taken hesitantly and with much doubt as to the wisdom of yielding to what had become a pressing popular demand.

The individuality of the author was not a matter of serious concern to old-time audiences. They cared only for the theme, not regarding critically, or even with any definite consciousness, its art or its source. Shakespeare was of so little account personally to his contemporaries and immediate successors that only the most scanty material for his biography survived him. The names of the greatest authors before the eighteenth century were familiar to a limited class of readers. Popularity was impossible. It was by soldiers and men of affairs that the prize of wide fame was won.

In eighteenth-century England, periodical literature was no longer confined to the narrow circle of erudite readers, but had become lively and entertaining to meet the keen demands of a polite audience equal in numbers to that which frequented the playhouses, and surpassing it in intelligence. The desire of genius for recognition in any honorable field is natural. Why, then, did the wits of Queen Anne's time seem to shun direct personal recognition? Why did Addison and Steele hide themselves behind the mask of "Mr. Bickerstaff"? Pope stood forth with bold effrontery, and, considering the freedom and sharpness of his relentless satire, he did not lack courage. His medium was verse, and he may have been more confident of success because nearly all his predecessors in English literature who had won enduring fame were poets.

But while the art of prose—of modern prose, at least—was then in its infancy, it was welcomed by an eagerly curious audience ready to appreciate its graces. A bright prospect was opened to such writers as were able to furnish urbane entertainment, this social service promoting also purely literary achievement, with a larger scope for individual authorship and individual aspirations. Why should this authorship seek a mask? It is not enough to say that masquerade was the habit of the age. The fact remains that individual authorship was but partially emancipated. Few writers could stand out in the open as Pope did, expressing themselves without fear or favor, having nothing to gain and nothing to lose. Satire was as much the weapon in letters as it was in politics. The mask served as armor.

The persistent hostility of the British government to the free expression of opinion in the press, as shown in oppressive taxation—such as brought the *Spectator* to an untimely end—and arbitrary inquisition, naturally drove the writer under cover and engendered timidity.

The profession of letters had not yet so far advanced in honor that simply excellence in its exercise would win either great regard or substantial profit. The "town" would yield its favor to such writers only as were effectively piquant or amusing. The attempt to win this favor was an experiment. The writer attaching his name to an essay would have seemed to count upon his success and to lack a becoming modesty. After he had won, the mask was likely to become transparent. "Junius" alone escaped this disclosure while he lived, and it is still a question who wrote the famous "Letters."

But even after the rewards of authorship in esteem and fortune were better assured, the mask still served the modest intent of the literary aspirant. In two instances—those of Chatterton and the author of "Ossian"—it was meant to be impenetrable

Generally, however, it was adopted as an expedient, shielding the experiment. Scott, when he began his career in the "Waverley" disguise, seemed to prefer his lairdship untainted by literature — at least by "scribbling" in prose—and only his remarkable success justified him to himself. His novels, with his own name on the title-page, would have had no element in them which could give the readers of them any special interest in his personality. As the great Unknown, this personality became intensely interesting and a challenge to curiosity. The mystery was unessential to a just recognition of the value of the novels, but it enhanced their immediate distinction and success. This element of mystery has since been availed of by "Boz," George Eliot, and many other pseudonyms, and sometimes through blank anonymity; and, for whatever reason the disguise has been adopted, it has always awakened additional interest, and so made it liable to suspicion as an artifice displacing natural modesty. Bulwer, in his discussion with Blackwood concerning the publication of his Caxton series of novels, after he had already become distinguished by his earlier fiction, seems to have deliberately chosen relapse to anonymity as of greater advantage than the name he had won.

We are inclined to believe that writers generally have attached very little importance to the exaltation of their names for their names' sake. It is not the seeing his name in print which causes the heart of the novice to rejoice, but seeing his work in print. Certainly he could not have seen his name in periodical literature until within a comparatively recent period. Now that he does see it, he is apt to look upon it rather deprecatingly as an unnecessary distraction from the work itself—a limitation upon it, a kind of impertinence. He feels that he must work hard and long simply to deprive that inert label of its insignificance. He sees other names which have lost this inertia, or whose inertia has become momentum in the race for glory, because they have been so long associated with work of the best sort, each with some peculiar excellence and quality— names which have finally come to live as distinct personalities.

If no names were given, the readers of the periodical, being without the guidance of labels, might not wait till they had supped with all their familiars before giving the new writer so much as a nod or a glance. They might even chance to favor him with their earliest attentions and partake of his little feast with unsated appetites.

So it was in the good old times. Then Charles Lamb felt as much at home in the pages of a magazine as at his own sheltered fireside. He would have shivered at the sight of his name in print as if he stood thinly clad in the wintry wind. "Elia" was a cheery, warm cloak to wrap about him when he wished to appear *en costume*. This extreme shyness would look like affectation in our day.

# THE PASSING OF ANONYMITY

There were considerations not due to modesty which made writers even in the early part of the nineteenth century averse to a direct acknowledgment of their contributions to periodical literature. The periodical, however successful it might have become, received rather than conferred dignity in its relation to its important contributors. The old stigma upon the literary profession itself still remained in such force that there was not one of the brilliant young men who started the *Edinburgh Review* but would have preferred to owe his reputation mainly to some other profession. Lockhart, after *Blackwood*, for which he had done so much, had achieved remarkable distinction as well as success, expressed his growing aversion to periodical literature, though he adhered to it, and was at the time about to accept the editorship of Murray's *Quarterly Review*. He had been familiar with this field as the arena of fierce political conflict and spiteful literary criticism, and was just then depressed by his own connection with the duel in which John Scott, the editor of the *London Magazine*, had been killed. It was not until the forties that literature and the literary periodical attained to anything like the full measure of their honorable recognition. Anonymity in the early years of *Blackwood* was often the refuge of libellers, whose assaults were only restrained by the liability of the publisher.

In those days, too, the publication of contributors' names would have disclosed the poverty of literature

—at least of literature both good enough and available. It was not an uncommon thing for Brougham
in the *Edinburgh Review* or Wilson in *Blackwood* to
contribute half a dozen articles to a single number.
Brougham is reported to have written the entire
contents of one number of the *Review*, including an
article on Chinese music.

The habit of anonymity, once established, persisted, and it may have outlasted its virtues as well
as its necessities and its vices. But we are not quite
sure that, in the interests of literature, it was wisely
abandoned. The urgent demand of magazine readers for the publication of names is easily accounted
for in an age which revels in personalities almost, if
not quite, to the point of debauchery. Names are
bandied about as mere tokens, with no reference
to the essential values which have made them significant or interesting. The banality of this habit
is conspicuous. The association of a writer's name
with his work is natural and proper. But the careful and thoughtful reader will, without the author's
name, build up his true personality from the individual traits disclosed in his work or in his manner
of work, and the really great writer thus discerned
becomes an important part of this reader's culture,
and along with this is developed a familiar and
friendly association, a haunting companionship. A
few such authors make for him an interesting world.
How different is his case from that of the reader who

requires the names of contributors that he may waste no time in finding out the distinctive traits to know an author by! He belongs to that polite world which has the common habit of conversation about books and pictures, with varying degrees of intelligence and interest; and he is expected to contribute his share to this kind of entertainment. He lives in a world of talk, of spoken and printed gossip, and thus acquires much knowledge about writers who are in vogue without any serious study of their work, for which he has as little time as inclination. He pays his passing tribute as a reader, and is sure to confine his attention to literary notabilities.

That loose liberality which excludes rational standards, which counts notoriety as a legitimate distinction, tends to degeneration. The temptation is offered to the new writer to win an easy success by getting himself talked about through some eccentric performance lying outside the range of literature. Henceforth his name stands for vast possibilities in his particular field of sensationalism, and has a commercial value beyond that of nearly, if not quite, all his worthy contemporaries, and becomes a temptation to many publishers.

The profession of letters deserves and commands a commercial profit. In periodical literature before the nineteenth century this was a comparatively insignificant factor. And afterward, in the early *Blackwood* period, when a circulation of six thousand copies was considered a triumphant success, the payment of eminent contributors was modestly disguised as an *honorarium;* the other contributors were "literary hacks" and were poorly paid. When fiction of the higher order became an important element in magazines, and when, later, the literary hack was, in the natural course of progress, excluded, the prizes of periodical literature rapidly increased —more rapidly in America than in England. The names of prominent writers, because they represented essential worth, had also, and legitimately, a corresponding commercial value. This element was recognized before magazines published names with contributions; distinction could not escape appreciation, and authorship soon became an open secret.

In this situation, the new writer shared with the older, and in proportion to his merit, the praise of readers. He had a fair chance. His peril, and the peril to literature, came with the use of names as potent in themselves, and with the assumption that they were the inevitable and indispensable condition of success. The most unfortunate circumstance connected with the immediate disclosure of authorship by the publication of the names of contributors is that the custom was adopted at a time when it seemed likely to do the most harm, by giving countenance to this unwarranted assumption.

Happily, the real effect of the perils we have mentioned—that of the substitution of notoriety for substantial distinction and that of the eclipse of intrinsic worth by the acknowledged omnipotence of names associated with success—has been only to more sharply draw the lines of selection in both book and periodical publications, but more especially in the latter, because, while the reader chooses what books he will buy, he does not share with the publisher the selection of articles in a magazine, except indirectly through his exercise of choice between periodicals. Therefore it is that the first - class magazines have become the principal safeguards of literature against its deterioration. It is comparatively easier for them to withstand obviously corrupting influences, by rejecting sensational or otherwise unworthy features, than it is to resist insidious temptations; and what could be more insinuating than the persuasiveness of a great name, the undiscriminating acceptance of which, without appraisal of the production which bears it, would be so readily condoned by a large body of readers? That is a good part of the difficulty—the necessity of guarding readers against their own easy acquiescence. Writers, too, have to be guarded against themselves — against the overbearing attitude of some of them who insist upon that unconditional surrender of the editor which encourages too facile and sometimes feeble accomplishment. It is not fair to the author—setting aside all other questions of fairness—to accept without consideration whatever he may, in any kind of circumstances affecting his production, have to offer, in response to the editor's expressed and genuine desire for his work.

Even commerce implies reciprocal benefits and obligations. The author who ignores editorial approval lends his authority to the prevalent assumption that it is the name and not the thing that counts, as the editor who allows himself to play the dummy in so important a transaction confesses to the truth of that assumption.

For ourselves, it is our habit as well as our choice to read every manuscript without any reference to the name of the writer, and to reach our decision upon it before we acquaint ourselves with that purely incidental and secondary fact. If, when our opinion is a favorable one, and we finally look for the name, we find that it is one we have never seen before, we experience that rare pleasure familiar to every editor who is capable of enthusiasm in the cause he maintains.

· How far astray is the new and unknown writer who fancies that he has no chance in competition with the favored expert! He little knows how eagerly his distinction of quality, if he has it, is welcomed, even in preference to the distinction of an established reputation. Only too easily is the old displaced by the new. The manuscripts submitted to the editor of any first-rate magazine—however many of them there may be—receive his earnest personal attention, lest by any chance the writer with the new note should escape his recognition. But, even after the recognition, there is the slow development of the new author's fruition. However sure the growth, it must be nourished. He becomes in time the old, the experienced author. His readers have grown with him; having been initiated by him into some new mysteries that could have been disclosed only by his magical power, they have waited upon him for new revelations with frankly avowed confidence and loving expectation, and they would not willingly have the revels ended or see him lay aside the master's wand. Younger writers, trying their wings, look up to him, taking courage from his bolder flight, which they emulate without envy. He is the elder brother in the fraternity of letters; even his characteristic faults are fondly indulged; no one so ill-natured as to wish him jostled aside to give place to any new-comer. We have seen them one after another, with different degrees of exaltation—Irving, Bryant, Longfellow, Curtis, Lowell, Holmes, Warner, Stoddard, Aldrich, and Stedman, who have passed away, crowned with love and laurels; and Howells and Mark Twain, who still graciously lend their strong presences to our living world of letters. Room for them? Yes, the Upper Room, where we spread our grateful feast for these who have had so long the freedom of our hearts!

It is not the new name that counts any more than it is the old one, with its cherished associations. The undiscriminating reader might as easily err in one extreme as the other. He might ask for a new deal in every one of a motley procession of numbers. It is the best things that are wanted in any number, whatever names may be attached to them, and, while we regard it as of the first importance to literature that the earliest expression of individual genius should be not only protected against any overshadowing weight of established authority, but be welcomed enthusiastically—as we believe it is by readers as well as by editors,—still it is not a case where we are off with the old love before we are on with the new. The magazine is a continuous culture, maintained chiefly by experienced writers, but ever reinforced and constantly lifted to a higher plane by those who certainly, if inexpertly, sound the note which is to be the dominant in a new harmony.

The demand for the publication of authors' names in the magazine of to-day has a rational justification because of the intimacy of writer and reader in our modern literature. We do not care for the personality of the showman when our attention is wholly absorbed by the spectacle. But when all other masks are renounced, and writer and reader meet on the same plane—each a sensible partner in the communication—why retain the mask of anonymity?

# CHAPTER IX

## PRIZES OF AUTHORSHIP

MUCH as we hear nowadays of the commercialization of literature, it is pleasant to reflect that great authorship has never been associated with unworthy motives. The manifestation of genius is so spontaneous than it seems amiss to speak of it as having motives of any sort. If in exceptional instances individual traits are disclosed which we deprecate or deem unhappy, the incentive to expression has been noble and ingenuous, free from the taint of mean and sordid considerations.

Shakespeare made stagecraft a profitable business—a fact which reflects credit upon his practical judgment,—but the quality of his poetic genius which made him immortal was distinctly manifest in what he wrote before he was known as a playwright, and, in any case, could not be commercially accounted for. Bacon as a writer could not have even had such temptations as beset him in his judicial office. Authors who were useful to their patrons have not by that utility laid claim to the greatness ascribed to them by their contemporaries or by posterity. Apart from the prizes of the theatre and the benefits of patronage, no writer, ancient or modern, before the eighteenth century, derived any substantial pecuniary profit from his work. Homer sang with ethnic enthusiasm, reflecting the brightness of the heroic past—as other epic poets have done for other races,—Hesiod, for a religious cult and an ethical purpose, and the later Greek poets for the perfection of their art and the glory of their respective cities. The Augustan age of Rome gave Horace his Mæcenas, Virgil the favor of the court, and both these writers something like what we moderns call publication. If they could not "see themselves in print"—as indeed no writer could before the time of Rabelais,—such personal vanity as they may have had derived no slight satisfaction from elegant copies of their poems, which they knew were also the possession and pride of their polite contemporaries. Dante, Petrarch, Boccaccio, and Chaucer had the same delightful experience. But their chief reward was in the recognition of a noble acquaintance, which they shared with Plato and all those greatest writers of antiquity who had suddenly come into their modern kingdom, passing from porch, academe, and forum into the studies of the learned and into the boudoirs of princesses and courtly ladies.

These lofty examples of genius might too easily lead us to false conclusions. Opportunity did not open any door to great writers for the exploitation of literature with sordid motives. Their memorable achievements only prove that such motives are not necessary for the stimulation and exercise of the highest powers. If political influence, official and social prestige, and such material benefits as may have attended them were not refused, we know that they were incidentally a reward and neither the lure nor the price of the supreme expression. For then, as always, the native attitude of genius toward merely material possessions was one of disdain or of mastery. We note even in the business world such an attitude as distinguishing the genius of organization from the common mercantile mind, wholly absorbed in accumulation.

In that long period when there was no popular audience for literature, the old aristocratic *régime* had full dominion, and even the exceptional genius, lifted from the lower ranks through patronage or through the opportunity for success in the theatre, was brought, with easy consent, into alliance with this order of things. The hireling and the trades-man were in contempt, and an injurious prejudice against them persisted long after the elevation of the middle class, through education and democratic revolt, so that when the publishing business began to exist as a distinct craft in the hands of Tonson and of his imitators and successors, the creators of a polite literature were for some time disposed to avoid or conceal relations with this new class of shopkeepers. The successful establishment of such a trade was possible for the first time through the support of a popular constituency. The popular periodical miscellany was sure to follow, but it was preceded by the essay serial, established on individual responsibility by the wits of the town, and appealing to the tastes of the elegant. The shop boldly asserted itself when Mr. Cave started the *Gentleman's Magazine*, and has held its own ever since, with ever-advancing dignity. Nevertheless, contributors avoided publicity, and those of the more distinguished class felt that some stigma was attached to any bargaining with the shopkeepers. Enterprising publishers of the next century, the Constables and Murrays and Blackwoods, encountered the same sensitiveness. Wilson and Lockhart made no pecuniary charge for years of editorial assistance to Mr. Blackwood on his magazine.

In this respect there was a marked distinction between the book and the magazine contribution. So long as the popular magazine continued to be mainly a miscellany, the book naturally seemed a more dignified form of publication, and its author obviously conferred a favor upon the publisher, who became his obedient servant in the business transaction. Though the writer, along with the greater dignity, obtained also a larger profit, the pecuniary reward was free from the taint of the shop. Dr. Johnson received more from his *Rasselas*, the work of a week, for which he was paid £125, than he

could have earned upon a magazine by the assidu-
ous labor of six months. As early as 1818 William
Blackwood paid Miss Susan Ferrier, then an unknown writer, £150 for the book rights of her
first novel, *Marriage*. For the second novel of this
author, who at once took her place alongside of
Miss Edgeworth and Miss Austen, portraying Scotch
society as vividly and with as much humor as
these had the Irish and the English, Blackwood
paid in advance £1000—this sum not including the
entire copyright. The costly editions of books,
though small, from our point of view, in the number
of sales—six thousand copies having been considered very fair in the case of the extremely popular
"Waverley"—netted very large profits.

What most surprises us in the comparison of
those times with our own is the high record of prices
for volumes of verse. Of course, the offer by Long-
mans of 3000 guineas to Tom Moore for "Lalla
Rookh," before that poem was written, was without
precedent, though it became one for prices afterward received by him. But Tom Moore was never
mercenary. It is recorded of him that he paid a
debt of several thousand pounds, incurred by the
error of his deputy at Bermuda, and refused a sub-
scription from Whig friends, headed by a young no-
bleman who afterward became prime-minister—Lord
John Russell.

For the "Siege of Corinth" and "Parisina" Murray

sent Byron his draft for £1000, which the poet returned on the ground that the poems were not worth so much, declining also the offer of £250 additional, which brought the payment up to the rate of £1 a line. Lord Byron finally yielded to Murray's importunity for the separate publication of the poems, the more readily because he was financially embarrassed; but his first resistance reflects credit upon his modesty as well as upon his judgment.

Pope had made £9000, nearly a century earlier, by his translation of Homer's *Iliad* and *Odyssey*. Mr. John Bigelow, in his *Life of Bryant*, compares the profits which the latter poet received from his version of Homer with those received by Pope in a very suggestive paragraph which throws light upon the diverse conditions of publication in these two epochs, two hundred and fifty years apart. In 1888—seventeen years after the completion of his translation—Bryant's sales had amounted to 27,244 copies, against less than 2000 copies of Pope's during a corresponding period. Yet Pope's income from sales was nearly three times as much as Bryant's, which amounted to $17,000. This is to be accounted for by the large number of volumes standing for a copy and by the higher price—a guinea a volume. "There is," says Mr. Bigelow, "a moral for publishers and authors in the circumstance that while 3283 copies of the more costly 8vo edition of [Bryant's] *Iliad* were selling, 5449 copies of the 12mo edition in two volumes were disposed of." The comparative royalties were, from the cheaper edition, $4713.60, and, from the more costly, $811.80.

The poets seem to have had their heyday before the middle of the nineteenth century, when poetry was superseded in the public interest by fiction. A poet making his first venture with a London publisher might, as Mark Akenside did with "Pleasures of the Imagination," accompanied by a commendatory word from Pope, get downright a copyright payment of £120. To-day an unknown poet would more likely be asked to guarantee the publisher in advance by himself paying from a half to three-fourths of that sum. Crabbe, with an introduction from Burke, was as fortunate as Akenside had been. Sustained poems of considerable length, like Beattie's "Last Minstrel," Campbell's "Pleasures of Hope," Gray's "Elegy," and Thomson's "Seasons," had a popular success and were profitable to their authors. Pollock's "Course of Time," written by a consumptive youth, who died in 1827, six months after its publication, reached in its second year a sale of twelve thousand copies, and for many years afterward was one of the most valuable of Blackwood's literary properties.

Some of these poets may have sent their first amateurish effusions to the *Gentleman's Magazine*, but we would look in vain to find even the briefest of their mature productions in such miscellanies. Moore and Wordsworth preferred to see their lyrics and sonnets in a good daily newspaper like the

*Morning Post*. The brightest essayists showed the same preference when they were not writing for periodicals of their own origination or such as were especially devoted to criticism. It was not till the advent of *Blackwood's* and the *London Magazine* that writers like De Quincey and Lamb or such a poet as Hood contributed to periodicals of a popular character. Dr. Johnson had in his time—half a century earlier—stood quite alone in this kind of service.

Conditions were rapidly changing in the publishing business, in the character of periodicals, and in the reading world. Books were not so dependent for success upon the patronage of subscribers. A frankly commercial relation existed between the author and the publisher, under regulations beneficial to both, and on the part of both there was an increasing appreciation of well-earned popularity. In the thirties, after the triumph of the Reform Bill, books were reduced in price, and there were cheaper publications—some of a wretched sort appealing to low taste, but others, like Knight's *Penny Magazine*, of an informing and improving character. It was in this period that the great London literary weeklies were established, after the type of the *Examiner*. Such writers as Leigh Hunt and Hazlitt, whose names suggest a brilliant group of their contemporaries, had then ample opportunity in the wide and varied field of periodical literature.

But the prizes in the field, though excellent, were not dazzling. Ten guineas a sheet for Coleridge was about the limit of Blackwood's remuneration to any author. This publisher distinctly declared that he never did and never would "hold out money in itself as an inducement to men of talents to write for 'Maga.'" His most distinguished contributors held the same exalted view of literature. The *Edinburgh Review* paid at first ten guineas a sheet, and rose gradually to double that sum. Jeffrey, who was the editor until 1829, would accept no unpaid-for contributions, fearing that the proprietors might otherwise favor a certain class of contributors.

America at that time had no monthly magazine to compare with *Blackwood*, and the pecuniary rewards of such literature as then existed were insignificant. When Bryant was contributing to the Boston *Literary Gazette*, he modestly offered his poems at two dollars apiece, but the editor, Theophilus Parsons, set a higher value upon them. Among the poems thus offered were several of his best. And this was seven years after the publication of his "Thanatopsis." The *North American Review*, at the time when Longfellow and Prescott were contributing to it, paid a dollar a page. This was the period in which American literary sensibility was so far in advance of American literary production that the periodical essays of Macaulay, De Quincey, and Carlyle were collected and published in book form by American publishers before a like distinction was conferred upon them in England. From this fact, taken in connection with the low prices paid to the most promising authors, it is evident that a true appreciation of literature is not necessarily indicated by a monetary standard.

The contrasting situation which is presented in our own time has come about naturally and inevitably, inasmuch as there must be commercial equilibration between values and prices; yet some unhappy reflections and misgivings arise in us when we consider the kinds of value which have to be allowed for in our contemporary estimate of literature. Our regret is only the more poignant when irrefragable arguments convince us that the distortion of what should seem to be a just perspective is also inevitable. Almost we ask, when we contemplate the present conditions of publication, has the salt of literature lost its savor for those who deal in it commercially and who are apparently responsible for these conditions, if anybody can be held responsible for tendencies confessedly inevitable?

It is within our memory that the only factors in the business of publication were the author, the publisher, the bookseller, and the reader. Of these, the old-fashioned bookseller, who knew and intelligently appreciated the books he handled, has been driven to the wall, and the mechanical system which has taken his place is blind to every value he recognized and eagerly aware of those values which to him had no significance, but which have now come to the front, determining through indiscriminate advertisment the choice of a fickle multitude of book-buyers. The record of big sales is paraded as in itself a certificate of merit. The relation of the publisher to author and reader has lost much of its former frankness and simplicity. The literary agent on the one side and the "trade" on the other seek to force his hand, and if they do not make him an out-and-out merchant, with an eye only to the market, it is because he has uncommon virtues of resistance. We are optimistic enough to presume that he may maintain a wisely chosen alternative.

We trust that we are catholic enough also to properly appreciate the claims of that vast sum of current literature, whether in books or periodicals, which, however evanescent, rests upon a solid and legitimate commercial basis and has relatively both use and worth, serving its day and generation. The newspapers throughout the country abound in this kind of writing, which, though modestly rewarded, gives an opportunity to many thousands for a wholesome and interesting exercise of mental talent; and not unfrequently out of this nursery emerges a notable author of a higher, if not of the highest, type. It is, in our opinion, a fortunate circumstance that there are so many books and periodicals which, while they do not appeal to highly cultivated readers, are yet stepping-stones to a loftier plane of intellectual and emotional satisfactions, and when a writer in this field through unusual talent wins large esteem and ample prosperity, we do not complain because he has not the brilliance of George Meredith or the charm of Howells. That commercialism of literature which secures such excellence and such rewards is an honor to civilization.

What we should deprecate is that meretricious commerce which lowers the standards of both life and literature by holding out money as the chief inducement to the exercise of genius or talent. No writer can do his best if his highest prize is not that of excellence, if the joy of his work is not his greatest satisfaction. This is the gospel of the kingdom of heaven in literature, and to the author who has this kingdom within him all other things are added that are of any real worth or can be worthily enjoyed. To him is given the high privilege of the society of noble minds—an immortal society continued from one generation to another—and of participation in its far-reaching aspirations, to which he gives form and utterance as a master-builder in its temple of beauty and truth. This society and its recognition of him is far more to him than any cheap fame or material emolument which more and more the market presses upon his attention, invading the temple itself. He has not only scorn for the sellers that offer him the world for his soul, but the scourge to drive them out.

The courage to maintain this position, ideal as it

may seem, is not so rare but that it has been the possession of every master in literature, even to the present moment. There are no names save of these masters to which the market itself has paid such perennial tribute. Cheap fame is short-lived, and sordid traders, well enough aware of this fact, make the most of the bubble before it breaks. The books of many of the greatest living authors, English and American, have seemed, on their first issue, to have small sales in comparison with those of far inferior writers; but they have continued to sell year after year, justifying the wisdom of their publishers. They constitute the literature of every well-ordered library. Even periodicals which have bid first of all for merely popular success eagerly offer such writers three or four times the liberal prices paid them by magazines through which their names have won world-wide familiarity.

The prestige of a magazine depends upon its quality—that is, upon its record for the maintenance of high standards in its literature. Popularity cannot confer it, any more than it can win for it that affection which goes with high esteem. One of the values of such prestige is that it attracts writers who care more for a distinguishing quality in their work than for its pecuniary reward. The contributor shares in the prestige and appreciates its worth to him. By the law which inheres in the fitness of things, a magazine of distinction can always afford to pay liberal prices, and it does not need to bid against others by tempting offers of money to its writers in order to hold them to a natural allegiance. Magazines of this class are becomingly proud of names which represent real distinction in the world of letters and association with which betokens noble alliances, but they would not wield the *brutum fulmen* of a name signifying merely phenomenal success for advertising purposes—would, indeed, rather repudiate altogether the possession of the name itself, as a title of ignobility.

The art of a writer justly entitles him to a recognition corresponding to the degree of its excellence; but for the uses of a periodical the excellence must be not merely technical — it must be that which secures appeal, compelling sympathetic response. The master *motif* is essential to all great art. The expert writer, with all his felicity of phrasing and the perfection of an exquisite manner, but as soulless as a faultlessly dressed model, should not complain that his faculty counts for so little even in comparison with the rough and halting expression of a writer endowed with the inward grace and native dignity of simple manhood. The power of appeal, reinforced by æsthetic charm, sets an author apart, and the prizes he wins, expressed in spiritual or material terms, are an accidental glory. Who is rich enough to pay him for his work? Who shall even make mention of fame in the presence of one who himself has the gift of the knightly accolade?

The wealth of a kingdom could not buy a single great poem. Here money is but a tribute to sovereignty.

It sometimes happens that a contributor honestly and without incurring the imputation of immodesty thinks himself insufficiently rewarded, comparing his own merits with those of other writers who, as he knows, receive higher rates. Thackeray, after he had by his *Yellowplush Papers* become the most popular contributor to *Fraser's Magazine*, very justly complained that other contributors were better paid, and struck for twelve guineas a sheet—not quite four dollars a page. That was seventy years ago. Different magazines of the same class vary in their estimates of particular values according to the variations determined by their own individual preferences, since each is in some way distinct from the others, and is willing to pay more for what it especially desires. Even in stories there is this distinction of individual preference. Sooner or later the writer finds his affinity, and the equilibrium is restored to the satisfaction of all parties concerned.

As with the advent of the monthly magazine an opportunity was for the first time given to writers, independently of their material circumstances or social condition, and even of their experience in the world of letters, to achieve in varying degrees, according to their powers, distinction and profit, so, in the progress of magazines toward a higher excellence in every department of literature, their contributors have been stimulated by more eager enthusiasm and a loftier literary purpose as well as by a larger hope of legitimate financial success. Writers of fiction have gained the greatest advantage through this medium of communication with an appreciative audience, their crude but promising early work preparing the way for brilliant triumphs. How many of these young writers would have fallen by the way, victims of inexorable circumstance, but for this encouragement!

The crucial test of a publisher's attitude, of his esteem for literature on its intrinsic merits, is his appreciation of a worthy unknown writer. He is willing, as such an author or contributor is also likely to be, to let the commercial success of his undertaking take care of itself, as something purely incidental. His faith is in the only readers he cares to have—those who can discern merit on its simple disclosure. There are in England and America a respectable number of publishing houses which have developed a corresponding faith in generations of readers, and the periodicals which they have established enjoy the same confidence. A new publisher, following their example, like the promising new writer, is sure of speedy recognition.

There still remains the quiet world of culture, whose garden ever grows. There all really great literature thrives in untainted prosperity.

# CHAPTER X

THE desire for fame, as a motive to literary expression, seems to us hardly worth considering, though it is generally assumed to be the strongest incentive, and the noblest, if it is an aspiration and not an ambition.

"The thoughts of the boy are long, long thoughts," and in this expansion of the youthful mind the prospect is as immense as the retrospect, and the future is thronged with as eminent personages, the creatures of his imagination, as the past is with those history has made him acquainted with. He is a part of this coming eminence, since it has no shape except in his own dreams, but the vista stretching out before him and his relation to it are as vague as his dreams are. What he is to meet is so different from what he feigns, after the fashion of the past, that whatever definite goal he may set before him is likely to vanish and the veil of his cherished vision to be broken the moment he enters upon his course.

No great writer has ever consciously striven for a

deathless fame. Such a writer is wholly absorbed in his work. Any vague desire he may have hitherto nourished is displaced by a distinct vision of beauty and truth which eclipses every ulterior object, demanding only and imperatively its own embodiment. Like Horace, he must be able to say "*Exegi monumentum*" before he exclaims "*Non omnis moriar!*"

It was in an essay showing the advantages of obscurity that Cowley said: "I love and commend a true, good fame, because it is the shadow of virtue, not that it doth any good to the body which it accompanies, but it is an efficacious shadow, and, like that of St. Peter, cures the diseases of others." The writer's immortality is not his own concern, but that of his posterity. To the student of literature it is of interest because the conditions which determine it are inseparable from those which determine the evolution of literature itself.

We have reached a stage in this evolution—have reached it indeed at the very point in time where we now stand—in which the conditions affecting an author's prosperity with his present audience, as related to that which he may hope for with any possible audience of the future, challenge our attention. We are witnessing the culmination of a movement which began two centuries ago and which marked a distinct breach with antiquity. It was initiated with the advent of periodical literature in popular miscellanies, a literary transformation through the diversion of genius into new channels, new modes of expression. It had an earlier cradling, since it was really due to an audience which had expanded beyond the limits of that society of the erudite hitherto addressed by select authors—the society for which books like Burton's *Anatomy of Melancholy* was written, and which had fostered pedantry in the best writers, off the stage, ever since there had been any English writing.

The wider audience consisted, on the one hand, of the elegant and refined who, since the Restoration, had welcomed poets like Herrick and Butler—the author of *Hudibras*—and Gay and Prior, and, on the other, of the common people, for whom Bunyan had written, and who had been educated under nonconformist and democratic influences. This audience demanded a more familiar communication, and periodical literature, heralded by the already successful newspaper and bold pamphleteer, assumed that office. But in this undertaking the periodical was very soon surpassed by the novel of English society, which in its earliest examples, from the pen of Henry Fielding, was far less antique than Doctor Johnson's magazine essays, and which, in its familiar appeal and idiomatic speech, inherited from the *Spectator*. The novel was then something quite separate from the periodical; when they coalesced in the next century they together finally accomplished the literary revolution which each had independently initiated.

The full effect of the transformation is apparent only in our own time, but, from the first establishment of ready channels for familiar communication between writers and a large body of readers, it is obvious that both writing and reading began to mean something different from what they had meant before. The modernity of literature has been developed along with that modernity of our life which has been intensified by the employment of steam and electricity for the annihilation of distance in space and time. The breach with antiquity was a departure, not from what we call the ancient and mediæval world—it came too late for definition in those stereotyped terms—but from an old order of life as well as of literature in which the people were supinely participant but had no initiative, no voice but that of assent. This order had maintained itself long after the Renaissance, and for more than two centuries after the discovery of America. Class distinctions had the fixity of established types, marked by clearly visible external insignia; letters and the fine arts were under noble patronage; the social organization of every realm was consolidated by military discipline and, impelled in every movement by arbitrary sovereignty, marched with processional regularity, as if keeping step to martial music: altogether a picturesque and impressive spectacle, in which monarchs and prelates and warriors shone with varied and conspicuous distinction. The harmony of the order itself was sustained, by whatever frequent and devastating conflicts the peace of the world was disturbed. Its stability survived those delimitations of empires which were forever transforming the map of Europe and Asia and, later, of America. The entire period of its existence was studded with Great Events, chiefly wars, and literature seemed mainly to be the reflection of these, from Homer's story of the siege of Troy to Addison's celebration of the battle of Blenheim. The writers whose renown is bound up with the splendors they reflected were for the most part poets, who kept step with that old processional.

When the people began to have a voice in public affairs and a popular audience began to determine the course of literature, making its demands felt there, the ancient *régime* was doomed, and a writer's renown came to depend upon his partnership with his readers—with their thought and feeling—as to both his matter and manner. His predecessors had shared the glory of the great ones of the earth, and their fame was that of a like spectacular eminence. Whatever greatness they had in themselves was recognized only by the few who still could read them, but their names shone forever in the literary heavens, remote and unassailable.

Such popular audiences as there had been in the old *régime* were not made up of readers, were indeed illiterate, listeners and lookers-on at stage representations, at forensic displays, and at stately political or religious functions. Whatever argument or theme there was in these, something for the ear and the mind beyond the visible spectacle and pomp, was familiar, not in the intimate appeal, but as relating to myths, sentiments, typical ideas, held in common, and dramatically or symbolically illustrated. The popular participation was simply that of response, however ready and enthusiastic, to an outwardly imparted traditional communication.

Now it was a mentally developed popular audience of readers, which compelled the participation of writers in its own world—a world which was growing away from mute dependency and becoming something on its own account. In eighteenth-century England it was a divided audience, a considerable part of which was still bound by old social traditions, and all of which, including even the non-conformist and democratic, was frankly conventional. But the very existence of such an audience was significant, connoting the beginning of a new era in literature, in which writers were divested of courtly attire and seen plain, submitting themselves to the estimate and near regard of a contemporary public.

Thus prose came into vogue and was developed at the expense of poetry. One hardly remembers the names of the poets laureate of that period. The popular periodical reinforced as well as initiated every characteristic feature of this prose development. It promoted the brokenness of literary structure, since brevity and variety were the necessary conditions of its existence and of its successful appeal to an audience demanding the short essay. We can understand why Burke was not a contributor to magazines, preferring to institute that massive year-book, the *Annual Register*, which he wrote himself and kept up from 1759 to 1788, finding through this medium full scope for the amplitude and elaboration of his splendid prose. But he had that intense interest in contemporaneous things which distinguishes the periodical, making it always the mirror of its time. The society novel, which in Fielding's time was far from brief, was wholly engaged in the portrayal of contemporary character and manners. The concentration of public attention upon affairs of the moment was a distinguishing feature of the century. The wit of Horace and the satire of Juvenal, revived in "Imitations," found their butts and victims near at hand.

The Romantic revival in the latter part of the century showed a strong tendency toward a reversion to older types, but it stopped short of antiquity, was more Gothic than it was, in a general sense, mediæval in its inspiration, was radically national, and, for the poets, was more Elizabethan than Gothic. The true character of the revival was apparent in the next century, after it had been relieved of its barbaric conceits, and Scott had concluded his picturesque historical revels. Two more Great Events had in the mean time been added to those which thronged the historical retrospect, but radically different from most of these—the war of American Independence, and the French Revolution, with its Napoleonic sequel; and it was these more than Romanticism which inspired Byron and Wordsworth and the poets of their time. In the clearing up after the storm eighteenth-century conventionalism had disappeared.

The *laudator temporis acti*, always with us, forever protests against the passing of the picturesque. The breaking up of the antique seems to him a corruption in our life and literature, as to the purists new locutions indicate corruption in our language. It does not appear strange that an author as well versed in Elizabethan poetry as Charles Lamb was should have exclaimed: "Hang the age! I'll write for antiquity." But Lamb and Leigh Hunt and Hazlitt were making a greater prose literature and for a wider, more eagerly postulant, and better educated audience than Johnson and Chesterfield were making a century earlier. Here, too, we find the periodical leading the way. It was the golden though brief period of the *London Magazine;* and *Blackwood's Magazine* and the *Edinburgh Review* were in the buoyant youth of their remarkable careers. The next two generations were to witness the full fruition of Victorian literature in its few great poets and its many great novelists, and at the same time a marvellous expansion of industry and commerce, fatal to the old-time leisure, filling the towns with human drudges and with the dust and soot and noise of factories, and awakening the indignant protests of Ruskin and Carlyle.

Then it was, midway in the nineteenth century, that prose rioted in its triumph over poetry—being especially rampant in the two authors just mentioned—monopolizing all its charms, save that of the measured line; and some of the poets—notably Whitman and to some extent Browning—broke up the very mould of their own art, as if envious of the freedom enjoyed by the prose masters. This preeminence of "loosened speech" is more evident in our day than ever before. It is not that the age has become prosaic or mechanical or from any decay of imaginative powers. On the contrary, it is the imagination which has been cultivated, and in lines leading away from its old devices—lines of revolt against artifice of every sort, metrical, rhetorical, dramatic, or even epigrammatic. In breaking altogether with antiquity we at last break with tradition and behold the truth of our human life divested of masks—that is, we behold it in its own investment and not in the old clothes put upon it.

We have come, then, in this extreme emancipation, to that art "which nature makes." The communication between writer and reader is not familiar through a symbolism traditionally imposed, but it has a new familiarity, made possible through the response of the developed sensibility of the reader to the creative faculty of the writer, so that the communication is immediate, as if in the light shared by both, flashed from the living truth itself. Only through that response is the disclosure completed. In this conjugation of minds in the world of the imagination, the participation of the audience is an indispensable factor, determining the prosperity of the writer, whose felicity is confined to such creative communication. The temple of fame is displaced by the house of life. The writer is remembered only so long as he is read. This has been true of authors for at least a hundred years. How different is their case as to perpetuity of fame from that of the great but seldom read authors from Homer to Pope!

In our characterization of the communication between the writer and reader of to-day as familiar, we have had in view the attitude which both have in common toward nature and human life—seeking a real comprehension of the truth in these. The old methods of mastery in literature have suffered no change save that determined by the sincerity of this quest. The world of man and nature is, as it ever must be, participant in every artistic communication and essential to its meaning—the harbor for all anchorages of the spirit. Objective embodiment is as necessary as ever; the accordant background, the atmosphere—every feature of a picture—but all for the psychical significance of the truth disclosed. The distinction of the new art from the old is that the world enters not as a contrived spectacle, and the picture exists for its reality, not for picturesqueness.

The more of the world there is in a story or in an essay which is a genuine creation of the imagination, the greater the interest, since the truth of life has thus an ampler interpretation in its natural complement, and the scope of human sympathy is enlarged. Other things being equal, it is upon a writer's knowledge of the world and his mastery of the art of faithfully communicating it that his influence and the extent of his recognition depend.

Science, therefore, within its limitations, which must always be narrower than those of literature, but which have been infinitely enlarged as compared with what they were in the eighteenth century, is a finer inspiration to the imaginative writer of our day than the most stirring of events ever could have been to his predecessors. What it was to Tennyson every reader of that poet knows. No other kind of knowledge has so impressed the minds of men with the conviction of the unity of all life and of a universal kinship which Wordsworth prophetically intimated. Science, within its limitations, not only yields real disclosures of the physical world, and thus confirms the quest of literature for truth in life, but has pursued its discoveries to the line of contact of the physical with the psychical, furnishing the imagination with luminous suggestions leading beyond nature's fixed cycles into the spiritual domain. It is not the materialism of science which could degrade literature, but a conventional materialism of our own fashioning.

Science is forever on the brink of some new mystery, and none of our old fables or fairy tales can match its romances. The proverb that truth is stranger than fiction—that is, than contrived fiction —has a fresh meaning not thought of in its making. Imaginative fiction entertains this stranger truth— the truth of evil as well as of good—following it without fear or disdain, whatever veritable shape it may take and whithersoever it leads.

This new order of communication is not a logical presentment of exact or absolute truth. The illusion remains. Nature has its own prismatic refractions of light, through the raindrops giving us the rainbow, and through the humid atmosphere the hues of the sunset sky. The illusions of life as presented in really great imaginative writing to-day are produced naturally, not artificially.

The prosperity of writers with readers of their own generation is no security for their hold upon posterity. In present conditions it would almost seem that the near regard is won at the expense of the future. By a strange paradox, individual immortality is denied to the writers of an age like ours, in which the individuality of each is so distinctive a feature. The old mask served for surer remembrance of an eminent author by posterity.

# CHAPTER XI

## POPULARITY

IF the popular audience has for two centuries determined the progressive phases of literature in
England and in America—ever since there has
been such a thing as American literature—why is it
that so many of our best writers seem to eschew
popularity?

This question concerns our immediately present
or emergent literature far more than it would have
concerned that of fifty years ago. The obvious, and
perhaps too easy, answer to it is that in the evolution
of literature there has been a specialization of both
writers and readers, inevitably dividing them into
classes with widely diverse tastes and interests. But
this specialization, though its ramifications have rapidly multiplied during the last two generations, as is
shown by the almost bewildering variety of periodical publications paraded on any typical metropolitan news-stand of to-day, was at least going on
in a clearly manifest course even much longer ago
than that lapse of time indicates.

It is within our memory—we might say almost

within the limits of a single generation—that great
writers have deliberately confined their appeal to
readers of advanced culture. It is a matter of special
note that Richardson's *Pamela* was generally read
by those who could read at all, and by every class
from the lady of quality to the chambermaid. We
accept the tradition, with such allowances as must
be made on account of the high price of books and
of the bourgeois prejudice against fiction. Certainly
there was nothing in the style of these novelists or
in their portrayal of life which could exclude them
from general acceptance, to which indeed they better
accommodated themselves than the superior artists
in fiction of a later time did. Scott, though he was
not so thoroughly human or, at least, did not treat
life as so plainly human, except when he was portraying the Scotch peasantry, erected no barrier
between himself and the humblest comprehension.
George Eliot, in her more homely fiction, and all the
great women novelists of her time who contented
themselves, as Mrs. Gaskell did in *Cranford*, with the
simple and faithful presentment of human life and
character, were popular writers.

When we come to consider the men who stood
foremost in fiction in the Victorian era and in the
later time, we find in them—with the exception at
least of Anthony Trollope and Mr. Howells—along
with strong mastery, a certain arbitrary masterfulness which, to one or another class of readers, has

interposed difficulty. Those of us who witnessed
the advent of Dickens can recall the antagonism of
a considerable number of readers, of good average
common-sense, to those novels which followed his
*Pickwick Papers*, and which took the world of
readers at large by storm. People who took life
seriously looked askance at his representations of
humanity, which seemed as unreal as those upon the
stage, and at the queerness and extravagant exaggeration of every detail. Even the names of his
characters excited aversion, illustrating the trifling
whimsicality of his whole dramatic procedure. The
readers who most enthusiastically accepted the overwrought humor and pathos of Dickens were, for
opposite reasons, apathetic to Thackeray's themes
and comment, which seemed to them tiresome as
well as trifling, while to the refined intellectual sensibilities these were more delightfully appealing than
anything in fiction since Fielding, who had been
even more masterful, in his satire, though with less
grace. Wilkie Collins and Charles Reade—the one
masterful in his invention, the other in his virile
handling—failed of that intimate sympathy which
the reader yields only to what is simply and convincingly real.

Yet all these men, with others whom we have not
the space to mention, had extensive popularity.
Readers differed in the kind and degree of their
esteem of them, but only as individuals, not by
classes. Thackeray came nearest to the exclusion

of the unpolite. Later, George Meredith, with aristocratic *hauteur*, forced that exclusion, and even, through individual peculiarities of style and method, made his fiction insufferably difficult to many of the polite. But he always had largeness of theme. Thomas Hardy, the greatest master of English fiction, presents no such difficulty, and has compelled all classes of readers. He is the pre-eminent living example, showing that neither the possession of genius nor the exercise of true art need impose any limit to general appreciation.

If we turn to other fields of literature, we find that the great writers of the last half of the nineteenth century most earnestly entertained and presented themes of vital interest to the whole human world. By poets like Tennyson and Longfellow and Lowell; by philosophers like Mill and Green and Spencer and Emerson; by essayists like Ruskin and Arnold and John Fiske, genius was held not merely as a high privilege, but as a trust.

Is there just cause of complaint against the new generation of writers on the ground that they fall short of these high aims?

It certainly cannot be said that the majority of these new writers are averse to popularity, when so many of them seem to have no other goal, outrivalling the political demagogues in their strife for the plaudits of the crowd, adopting indeed the same watchwords. There is no lack of strenuous fiction antagonizing every known abuse of our time—there never was more of it—to say nothing of many other forms of antagonism in the daily, weekly, monthly, and quarterly periodicals. It is a crusade, involving a large proportion of current literature.

The only point in the charge which has force is that the best of our new writers seem inclined to avoid any close touch with the large body of the people, surrendering the field entirely to their inferiors, while they devote themselves to the culture of an exquisite art and to the entertainment of a polite audience. It is not expected of them that they should bid with others for popularity or even directly espouse special causes, but only that they should cherish ideals which refine and uplift all society, and should so embody these in their noble art as to win popular sympathy. They need not degrade their art, but their themes should intimate that kind of beauty and truth which is remote from no human sensibility. Is it not just this that Tennyson meant to express in the conclusion of his poem, "The Palace of Art"?

We were about to say apologetically for our new writers that they are of course also young writers, and we look to maturity for the widest and deepest sympathy. But immediately the reflection is forced upon us that it was the earlier work of most of their elders that was most inspiring to the popular mind and heart. *Daniel Deronda* could not mean to the common people as much as *Adam Bede* meant, or *Scenes of Clerical Life*. How often it happens that with the development of a writer's art he comes to dwell in a more select neighborhood, sequestered from the common regard! Instances of this seclusion only too readily come to mind. But we have the contrary instances of novelists like Thomas Hardy, Mrs. Humphry Ward, Sir Gilbert Parker, and Margaret Deland, whose latest fiction has evoked the largest popular response, thus showing that even great sales are not incompatible with intrinsic excellence, and that there exists a really thoughtful and appreciative audience much more extensive than the fastidiously æsthetic writer or critic supposes—and more worthy of a master's consideration, because that portion of it which exceeds the narrow limitations so arbitrarily set makes the greatest exaction upon his creative powers. The work is worthier which meets the exaction.

The most exquisite art without largeness of theme lapses into dilletantism, which is encouraged by a small, idle, *boudoir* audience, asking only for light entertainment. The extreme opposite of this audience is the vulgar crowd which also demands entertainment only, through sensational excitement and, whatever the theme, through the crudest art. Between these extremes lies the imaginative writer's real audience, variously constituted according to differing tastes and degrees of culture, but united in its insistence upon substance rather than upon form, regarding the theme, indeed, as the most essential thing in art. It would be a supremely magical compulsion—far beyond that of Du Maurier's *Trilby* —which would give to any book absolute control of every part of this audience.

The diversification is not, as formerly it was, into distinct classes of readers, but is the result of a highly developed individualism. As the writers, who themselves emerge from this audience, are differentiated by the same individualistic development, their affinities are determined by a natural selection; but appreciation is so catholic that the intensity of admiration for a "favorite author" yields to at least the tolerant acceptance of others, in a wide range of varied distinction.

As a whole, this large body of fairly well-educated readers has been emancipated from certain traditions. A writer to-day could not count upon an audience for a novel based upon a protest against any particular form of creed; and he would have still less chance with the morbid religious sentimentalism which gave popularity to *The Wide World*. The silly love-romance so much in vogue fifty years ago would now generally seem positively distasteful. The old-fashioned didactic novel has no longer any audience. The mock-heroic, the morbid, and the obvious have disappeared from respectable contemporary literature. Faith and romance have not therefore vanished, nor has their everlasting alliance with creative imagination been broken; they have been born again into that new truth and beauty which genius itself realizes in its own renascence.

Conduct, Matthew Arnold said, is three-fourths of our existence; as the ostensible vestiture of human life, it is all of it that is visible. Didactic discourse cannot alter the springs of human action. The great novelist touches these hidden fountains, not by precept or by juggling with old formulas, but through living embodiments which appeal to sympathy rather than to formal judgment. It is this sympathetic quality in the treatment of life which especially distinguishes contemporary fiction, excluding the old satire which was so easy, and seemed so forceful, but was, after all, arbitrary and superficial. The new method is more deeply spiritual—is it any the less truly moral?

Inevitably, imaginative literature, in its most recent development, seems in some respects shorn of its old strength. The good and evil, blended as they must be in any true portrayal of our human nature, have no such dramatic presentment as when they were arrayed against each other in mortal conflict. The elimination of unadulterated hatred and downright malice from the conventionally cherished villain of the play spoils the effect expected in the *dénouement*. Almost entirely, too, the dramatic incident, as the turning-point of the story, leading

～so directly and easily to an effective adjustment of conditions which in the ordinary course of our real life are apt to prove hopelessly intractable, must be surrendered, and with it that objective impressiveness which the inferior craftsman readily turns to his advantage.

Our advanced novelist seems unduly handicapped at the start, having at his command, apparently, only an equally advanced portion of the vast intelligent audience which is now eagerly awaiting the master of its thought and feeling. Really it is due to the fault of his choice or to his lack of adequate genius that mastery is not his, in proportion of his own greatness, and without the sacrifice of any true principle of art. This audience is not willingly reactionary. It cannot, or the great majority of it cannot, breathe the rarefied air of that exalted region to which too many of our best writers retire, making much of "art for art's sake." Some who do not thus wilfully exclude themselves and who are most catholic in spirit yet hold themselves in leash, with excessive reserve suppressing impulse until it atrophies, while the people need the full sunburst of their genius.

Imaginative literature, for English speaking peoples, lacks the inspiration of stirring outward events such as had poignantly heroic significance to former generations. The struggle for civil and for religious liberty is no longer martial. We have no drum-beats and witness no processions of martyrs to the stake or the scaffold. The emancipations of the human spirit go on peacefully; and while they often involve agitating inward conflicts, they are not outwardly impressive. With this retirement from the extreme scenic projection, the novelist shifts the stress formerly given to the plot to a series of situations whose dramatic effect is quite entirely of a psychical character. His temptation is toward a complete retirement where he has recourse to analysis with a view mainly to the intellectual satisfaction of his readers or to an exquisite æsthetic satisfaction through the supple play of his fancy. But while he is forced to deny himself so much, he need not deny himself the whole throbbing world outside; indeed, the more he admits that world, with comprehending sympathy, the more effective will be his art and the wider the popular response to it. What effects may be secured, and in how wonderful variety, may be seen in the fiction—the short stories or serial novels —of a first-class periodical. This kind of periodical has reinforced the tendencies of the new art, with all its renunciations of merely outward impressive effects, but it has also saved it from degenerating into the production of an anæmic and disembodied literature.

Neither the best periodical literature nor the writers who are making it deliberately evade popularity. It is just here that we see most clearly how far the specialization of literature corresponds to the specialization of culture in the popular audience. No one can deny that an imperative obligation compels certain magazines to maintain the most advanced standards, and that any relaxation in this respect involves corruption for which there can be no compensating advantage—certainly none in the interests of literature. Here a limitation is evident. But are we not apt to be mistaken, when we consider it a fixed limitation, when we attempt to determine the capacity of the audience, apparently inaccessible to such magazines, to appreciate the best. Let us to a magazine otherwise of the highest quality add the attraction of pictorial illustration equally excellent. The audience is at once multiplied threefold. There has been no lowering of standards. The increased popularity is not due to the fact that pictures are of necessity more interesting than the text can be, but it is significant as showing a natural demand for the visualized embodiment, the definite objective projection not usually attained to in the text. Some story-writers reach a degree of visualization that makes pictorial illustration superfluous if not impertinent.

But there is possible to such periodical literature and books as sustain the loftiest standards of art a much greater expansion of popularity through a larger appeal. Here we confront a positive condition: that which determines the technique of the literary art, while it is indispensable, is negative. Here, too, the magazine, the book, and the audience wait, as perforce they must, upon the genius of our best imaginative writers.

Some great masters of the past who have come under the harrow of our advanced criticism had at least the excellence of their defects. Shall those new writers who accept—as indeed they must and ought—the dictates of this criticism simply or mainly show the defects of their excellences?

Why is it that the sales of Dickens's works, in England alone, amount in a single year to more than those of any later novelist during his whole lifetime? The readers of these novels do not lack intelligence, and a good number of them are of a sufficiently advanced culture to detect his faults. But whatever the higher criticism may disclose against him, there still remains the fulness of his robust human sympathy and that mastery of genius which holds the mind even of children, as that of Shakespeare's does.

We do not want another Dickens. We are willing to turn him over with that other old playwright, Shakespeare, to the tender mercies of Tolstoy. But we look, surely not in vain, for writers who shall weave the very substance of the great human drama into their fiction, as all the great masters have done, in whatever stage of the art.

# PART II

## THE NEW LITERATURE

# CHAPTER I

## PAST AND PRESENT

COMPARATIVE estimates of different periods in the literature of any people are apt to be misleading, and never more so than when the present is contrasted with the past. Often, as in the case of Greek literature, the remote past seems brighter and fresher than all the aftertime. The Homeric poems seem indeed so incomparable with anything in literature and art as to belong to neither. In truth, they do not belong to either. As the first myths are the spontaneous creations of a plastic imagination, so the early epic is the product of the imagination reacting upon the legends of heroic deeds, and is thus representative of the race type rather than belonging to any particular department of its development. Sometimes, as among the Finns, there is no significant sequel in the national growth, and the marvellous epic stands alone, the single manifestation of a people's genius.

No Greek ever thought of comparing Æschylus with Homer, although he was the master of a more developed art. It must be borne in mind that the

Homeric like the great Hindu epics, as we know them, were the products of civilizations far in advance of those which produced the Kalevala or the Nibelungenlied, and that a long way behind them was the morning, the creative font of the myths and legends which enriched them. Homer was not wholly unsophisticated. But to the Hellas of the fifth century B.C. he stood at the gates of Dawn, and was, moreover, invested with all the glamour of the Heroic age. The great Hellenic tragedians modestly confessed that their plays were only crumbs from Homer's table, and it is true that their themes were in the main borrowed from him. But their operation—that for which we esteem them and which won the plaudits of their contemporaries—was in a field a world away from Homer.

Hardly more than a century later than Æschylus the great orators of Greece flourished, Thucydides lifted history into the realm of art, and Plato laid the foundations of speculative philosophy. New conditions incident to the enlargement and deepening of human thought brought into exercise new activities, developed new qualities, and disclosed a new order of excellences. Doubtless many critics in this advanced era regretted the past glories of a former and mightier generation. Already Euripides, then self-exiled from Athens, wise and complex before his time, had at once worried and fascinated an audience upon whose sensibility he had been over-exacting, and in whose minds his plays must have suffered by comparison with the simple grandeur of Æschylus and the perfect art of Sophocles, though of this celebrated triad he was the greatest poet. Aristophanes, who in this period was at his best, had a richer and freer fancy than any other Greek poet, but in the critical estimate of his contemporaries he would have been dwarfed when contrasted with Pindar. If we go a little further ahead in time so as to include Aristotle, this age had more influence upon human thought than any other in the history of ancient civilization.

In the evolution of human culture as in that of the physical universe every advance involves at the same time a sacrifice of elemental force and a gain in structural excellence. It is in the lowest orders of organic life that the creative quality of that life is most conspicuous. So in literature the obvious and striking instances of creative power pass, giving place to a higher and more complex organization in which that power is veiled more and more in the progressive course of culture. Also, when the human imagination is most potently creative—that is, in the primitive and most plastic stage of the evolution —it is in its operation, whether of myth-making or of rhythmic expression, the movement of the mass rather than the manifestation of individual genius. No later manifestation can seem so nearly a divine operation as this. What is more marvellous than the genesis of a language?

Yet we would not call back into being these pre-historic wonders or those of the Homeric renascence —not those, indeed, of any age preceding our own —for our immediate delectation; we are quite well satisfied with such splendors as they show in our backward view, while enchanted by their very remoteness.

Since the beginning of the individualistic development, which has been mainly Indo-European, and the first impulse of which was Hellenic, a few eminent writers stand for the times in which they lived—for their limitations as well as for their advantages—and because of the durability of manuscript and of the printed page, though much has been lost, enough of their writings remain to us for our just estimate and appreciation. There is not one of them we would willingly lose from the retrospect, though for many a previous age whole groups of them have been eclipsed, sometimes by wilful neglect, but more often by fateful oblivion. Whatever Dante may have meant to Chaucer, Spencer, and Milton, or to such prose writers as Jeremy Taylor and Sir Thomas Browne, he certainly meant nothing to Dryden and Addison, to Goethe or Voltaire. During the distinctively mediæval period the great writers of Greece and Rome were hidden behind the barbaric veil; and, in turn, the wonders wrought inside that veil—the cathedrals, the chansons, the lyrics of troubador and minnesinger, the Nibelungenlied, the poems of the Elder Edda, the heroic romances, and the mystery plays—were ignored in ages illuminated by the revival of ancient culture, until the remarkable reaction at the close of the eighteenth century drew aside the veil and disclosed and magnified these wonders as a new inspiration to the imagination. In what is called the Augustan age all the great Elizabethan dramatists, except Shakespeare, and all the great poets who wrote before the middle of the seventeenth century, except Milton, were nearly obsolescent. Even Spenser was scarcely read. Until the middle of the eighteenth century Shakespeare was but a *nominis umbra* on the Continent.

Our own age, including the last two generations, may be said to be the only one which has the complete retrospect within the range of its clear vision and catholic appreciation. In another way the whole past is peculiarly ours—that is, as a part and not the mere background of our culture. We have no present inseparable from this past. Yet there is a present which, as something which is passing into the future, has a note of its own so distinct and independent as in one sense to exclude and repudiate the past—that is, denying it place as something standing alongside, as an explicit factor in what is going on.

Such is our indebtedness to the past that we are never inclined to boldly enough assert this exclusiveness. We would not welcome Spenser's *Faerie Queene* as a poem of to-day. Plato's *Republic* or

Sir Philip Sidney's *Apologie for Poetrie* or his *Arcadia* would fall upon dull ears for any present appeal. Scott's romances, widely as they are read, for the romantic interest that endures, would be no more welcome as present productions than Milton's epics or Sir Thomas Browne's *Religio Medici*. All the great works of the past which we delight in as past would as works of to-day encounter resentment, as things born out of their time.

Imaginative values are everlasting, but every age has its own form and costume which seem alien to another, and are only tolerated out of their time because of the essential excellence which they invest.

The merely outward costume and custom are attractive to us when reproduced for us in painting, play, or story, because of their novelty and picturesqueness, but we would not suffer them in the familiar intercourse of every-day life. Even the graceful minuet of the eighteenth century does not win its way with us except on the stage or as a contrived spectacle. For sacred uses, where tradition dominates, older architectural styles are maintained or revived, but for the ever-changing homely uses Gothic and Queen Anne and Georgian houses have the remoteness of a spectacle, save as they have endured in their own settings and their old associations, or in their adoption have been transformed by the spirit of our time.

But the style of a writer is something nearer to his individual spirit and to the spirit of his time than any outward form. It cannot pass from age to age (an age in this connection, of course, not being limited to a generation) and still seem native to the time. Whatever its heritage of precious possessions, every age has its own work to do, creatively. No new time can give us another Dante or Shakespeare, or even another Scott.

If in some ways we of to-day seem less than those who have preceded us, in many ways we are more. If we do not loom up in so singular and striking eminences, we strike deeper and have a broader vision. Culture with us seems to be developed largely on the side of our sensibility. We are quickly receptive of those impressions which are direct and vital, and have tempted writers to meet us on this ground—to break up old forms, to give up old affectations and mannerisms, and, while keeping and even multiplying the veils of art and the illusions of romance, to dispense with masquerade. We invite a more spontaneous and less ornate speech and a less sententious criticism. Our most esteemed writers have more real simplicity than Addison, whose elegances, natural for his time, would repel us as artificial.

Mr. Alfred Austin thinks the cultivated English audience of to-day less intellectual than that of Pope's time; but we doubt if at any time, in England or America, the intellectual sensibility of cultivated people has ever been as profound, sane, and catholic as it is in this generation. Fortunately we do not know Pope's *Essay on Man* by heart, or much give our hearts to it, anyway. Did any English poet ever have a wider or heartier appreciation than Tennyson? What is the meaning of the growing popularity in England of Matthew Arnold's poetry?

Is there, as the Poet Laureate asserts, "a growing distaste for the higher forms of poetry"? We have two kinds of intellectual satisfactions, and each is quite distinct from the other. That satisfaction which we derive from the masterpieces of the past (including even Pope's "Essay") is so complete that we do not hunger for their repetition in the present. We are just as eager for the new wine, though we do not want it in the old bottles. As to poetry, our cellars are so full of the old wine, pressed from every vintage under heaven and of all time, that we do not make so strong a demand upon our writers for poetry as for good prose, the quintessential virtues of which are a modern discovery. We think that the extensive appreciation of new novelists like Mrs. Humphry Ward and Maurice Hewlett is a very satisfactory test of the intellectuality of our period.

## CHAPTER II

### WHAT IS REALITY?

IN our day we note a tendency which has become a movement in full course. We read a novel by Hewlett or Conrad or Hichens, or such short stories as Muriel Campbell Dyar and Georg Schock are writing, and we say that these belong especially to and illustrate this growing tendency. We observe a similar movement in all forms of imaginative literature—a movement toward reality in our knowledge and portrayal of life.

Everything in the world and in our life is coming to be interesting to us only as seen plain. We cherish real knowledge rather than notions, escaping, as far as we may, the tyranny of our intellectual concepts and fancies and the entanglements and pitfalls into which our sophistication betrays us. Science, in its quest of reality, has registered the general progress toward emancipation. Philosophy is following the example of science.

In reading Professor William James's book on *Pragmatism* we seem to be led along very much the same course which we suppose Mr. Howells might take if he were to write a book on Realism in Literature. This does not introduce a new method into philosophy, but it is the first elaborate exposition and justification of an attitude toward truth, in the consideration of philosophic problems, which has hitherto been somewhat apologetically adopted.

In science it was long ago inevitable that the close investigation of phenomena should exclude all speculative pretensions. Such assumptions as were from time to time made concerning unknown substance back of known phenomena—such as the postulation of the atom and of the ether—were held not as certitudes, but merely as working hypotheses which would be given up for others after they should have served their turn. There was a time when mere classification gave satisfaction, as in botany and physiology before biology became a study of the cell. To name a thing and fix its place in a rational order was sufficient. Now such knowledge is accounted superficial, though its attainment involves careful and accurate observation; we are no longer satisfied with an orderly description of the world without us or within us; we desire to apprehend the real procedure of a genetic evolution, and, instead of leaping forward to a generalization which will enable us to label and shelve, and so summarily dismiss, the subject of our study, we linger with particulars and seek beginnings rather than conclusions.

Philosophy has naturally more tolerance of loose

vesture, priding herself on generalities. But science has forced her hand. Mr. James delights in bringing her down from her aerial heights to the ground; and the ground itself is exalted, just as our earth was when she was admitted to the celestial sisterhood without favor or prejudice. The abstract ideal to which we fly, escaping reality, ceases to have those virtues which we hoped to find in its tenuous atmosphere, and which, after all, are sensibly apparent to us only as we dwell in the real.

Mr. James is himself too much of an artist—as indeed he shows himself to be in the grace and charm of his literary expression—not to find the concrete in its "local habitation" more interesting than any notional entity. The universe may be One, as indeed is implied in the name we give it—but it is attractive to us chiefly because it is also Many, having begun to be charming with its passing from the homogeneous to the heterogeneous. It is significant that the æsthetic Indo-European at first imaginatively preferred polytheism, or favored a dualistic control of the universe by good and evil powers engaged in perpetual conflict. We are not ourselves seriously disturbed when we discover that heat may overcome gravitation, to which we impute universality, and do not need the consoling assurance—if it is consoling—that, at absolute zero, gravitation would probably be the only force in evidence; since the reduction of all things to a point below any temperature whatever, while it would convincingly

illustrate monism by a general and disastrous uni-
vertence, would also involve the extinction of life,
and thus of all the values we naturally cherish.

We agree with Mr. James that we prefer things as
they are, with such hopes as progressive pragmatism
will permit us to entertain of general issues. If there
is any far-off "divine event toward which the whole
creation moves," we certainly cannot wish it to meet
the rational expectations of what the world ought to
be or of what from the beginning it ought to have
been—a world of absolute completeness, in which
nothing should be left to desire or to attain.

All this is simply saying that we cheerfully accept
reality in whatever way it concerns us—in our life,
our philosophy, our science, and our literature.

Passing directly to literature, let us consider what
limitations the exclusion of unreal matter has imposed upon the imaginative writer as to the themes
at his command in his appeal to an audience which
demands only the real. There still remains a vast reactionary audience composed of people who have not
themselves, in the evolution of character, become
simply plain men and women, and who cherish in
their vague fancies the insignia of an order irrecov
erably past. Marble halls still haunt their dreams
inhabited by crowned princes and helmeted knights
and other very imposing personages; and all this
masquerade is the more hungrily sought after by
those from whose ordinary ways of life it is most

remote and by starvelings whose fantastic appetites long for better bread than can be made of wheat. Writers of romances have never been lacking to respond to the fancied needs of this class of readers, not only giving them the coveted foreign satisfaction, but also meeting nearer and more intimate cravings for abnormal mental and emotional nutrition.

Doubtless, too, we are all reactionary, of set purpose, now and then, taking a kind of holiday in spontaneous revels and masquerades, or allowing ourselves to be carried off our feet by some antique obsession, lest we take ourselves too seriously in our insistence upon plain clothes. It is a healthy reaction, because we know what we are about. Moreover, we may be sincerely retrospective, and the outworn antique may hold for us a resource beyond that of mere amusement when we reflect that what seems so unreal to us was in its own time intensely and often pathetically real. Even the pompous and picturesque past thus remains to us our legitimate though not negotiable possession.

Realism holds us mainly to what is contemporaneous, because present values are reckoned in current coin; but we are not denied historical romance, provided it be true history and genuine romance.

Nor are we absolutely forbidden the melodramatic, even off the stage, certainly not that species of it which is so much an element in our lives that in assuming its obsolescence we elude reality. Passion is profoundly real for all of us, and the exaltation which culture gives it, relieving its elemental violence, while happily unable to reduce its expression to logical terms, makes it a more interesting as well as a more respectable factor in literature than it was in an older time; and melodrama, in so far as it inherits the virtues of this rehabilitation, maintains its appeal. Impassioned prose, also, when free from rhetorical artifice, may reflect deep reality, though in our day it is likely to have a less elaborate expression than in the pages of De Quincey. Lofty themes, therefore, concerning matters of deep and everlasting interest to every human soul, have not lost their place in literature, though held more closely within the limits of a secure but mobile anchorage —secure because of its mobility—and always repudiating the Preacher's assurance that any position taken is the conclusion of the whole matter, whereas it should be but the beginning.

The chief value of realism is that, while it seems to bring us down to earth, it at the same time, as we have said, exalts the earth, so that the common and homely things have a new disclosure of old but neglected values. We accept our dwelling-place and find it glorified, so that we no longer in ungrateful contempt speak of home as exile. Other-worldliness waits its other-world. Our existence here is doubtless, if not exile, at least a sequestration, but we make the most of our enclosure—a garden of it, if we will. Nothing is in our intellect before it is in our senses, yet we find no good reason for disparaging our sensations because of this limitation. Embodiment is the very sacrament which the spirit has sought with all its desire, itself shaping that organism which is at once its confinement and its expansion.

Reality, then, is not distinguished from appearances, which are indeed realization. The soul in us is, through sensible phenomena, brought into closer correspondence with the souls in things, which are akin to our own, than through our intellections.

Realism in imaginative literature means closer relations with nature in all the phases she presents to us, and the writer abides with them and makes the most of them in all their chromatic variety, becoming unliterary in his immediate regard of them for their own sakes. But, whether poet or essayist or novelist, he makes human action and passion the dominant interest in this environment. Writers have always done this, but not always in this real way as to both natural and human phenomena.

We are aware that what we are insisting upon must seem like a truism to many of our readers, who ask if to portray life truly has not been the aim of all novelists. Did not Fielding speak of human nature with authority as if he were its infallible hierophant? And Samuel Warren, the author of *Ten Thousand a Year*—did he not regard himself as a successful rival of Dickens because of the reality of his fiction? Was not Defoe the father of realism, as he was, in a

way, of English fiction itself? Yet there is not one
of our critical readers who could not convict every
man who wrote novels before Thomas Hardy of unreality in the kind of thing which he attempted to
represent as human life, if not in his manner of
doing it. Many of the women who have written
fiction have come far nearer to realism, as we understand it, than the men; because they have been
content to present common things and common experiences in a plain and direct appeal.

Those who regard fiction as mainly a comment on
life naturally remind us that human nature is essentially the same in all ages, and that the views of
life entertained by the novelists of to-day must be
very much the same as those held by their predecessors. But it is just these "views" which realistic
fiction must more and more repudiate. Every observant man's mind reacts upon what he sees in the
world about him and what he finds in books, and
inevitably his generalizations crystallize into views.
That is what theory primarily means—a view. And
it is true that these views of life do not suffer much
change from one generation to another, for the purposes of didactic comment. But reality, as we have
intimated, rests rather in the particular than in the
general, in the individual rather than in the type, in
phenomena themselves rather than in any laws of
conduct we may deduce from them. George Eliot's
Mrs. Poyser is more spontaneous, less easily account-

ed for logically, than her Daniel Deronda, and is more genuinely interesting because more real.

Our sensibility as a factor in art and literature is susceptible of constant development from age to age. Color and tone to the eye and ear of the modern painter and musician are divided into distinct shades which were not apparent to their primitive forebears. Formal and applied ethics as stated in general terms were the same in the oldest Egyptian dynasties as in our own day. Our advance is in the field of our perceptions, in our real knowledge through physical and psychical sensibility simultaneously developed. Richard Jefferies revelled in a world of reality undreamed of by Pliny or Humboldt. Real, as distinguished from formal, ethics has had a corresponding development into the complex and infinitely varied phenomena of what we call our manners—our psychical physiognomy, the most subtle and elusive as well as the most spontaneous manifestation of our life which the creative artist has to interpret. It is a vital development not definable in any formulary. Considering this ever-widening field of reality, we begin to see what realism in imaginative literature means and how inadequate must be any definition of it through what it excludes or through some partial though very important positive characterization of it—one so important, for example, as its exaltation of the commonplace. One of the most misleading distinctions of it is that which opposes it to idealism. It is in reality only that beauty and all that is ideally excellent are embodied forth or brought home and made familiar.

Accurate observation of nature is necessary to scientific research and statement, but in imaginative writing it is not the description of the external world that is essential, but the feeling of it as a familiar complement of our humanity; yet the feeling must be as true as if it were born of real acquaintance. In like manner the human sympathy of the writer rather than his critical judgment will lead him into the true vision of human life. He does not make a photographic transcript of actualities which he has observed. His portrayal of human nature is creative; his characters are born, not fashioned or invented, else they and what they do and feel would seem unreal.

Realism enlarges instead of narrowing the writer's field of creative work. Life is the theme—not what we think about it, but what it discloses to our developed sensibility. The theme divides itself as the living itself is divided to us and among us, and not, as in the old didactic formularies, into "firstlies" and "secondlies," till we reach the "finallies." This real distribution develops surprises as novel as those fairy tales of recent science which are incidental to the disclosures of the universal life in its unfolding, which is a like dividing of itself to our comprehension. Following these lines, literature shows its unlimited resources for an entertainment far more interesting, if not so stately or imposing, than it could furnish under its old masks.

The enlargement of literature, like its enrichment, must be through the truth, which discloses the real values of our earthly existence and experience in their living terms, and which gives to common things and associations their full meaning, investing them with their natural pathos and with the romance formerly associated mainly with what was alien and remote. A new and higher kind of curiosity has been awakened and developed which the stories of old travellers like Marco Polo could not satisfy— a curiosity concerning intimate things. Our perspective is changed, diminishing the enchantments due to distance, as the microscope has outmatched the telescope in the revelation of the wonderful.

Any solicitude, therefore, which we may feel as to the immediate future of literature is not whether writers for the new generation will do the things which once seemed great, but whether they will still further widen the range of the human imagination in the field of reality. It is in that way that their larger appeal must be won.

# CHAPTER III

## CREATIVE VALUES IN LIFE AND LITERATURE

IT is the mild season in literature. A century ago the dynastic and revolutionary conflicts which agitated Europe were reflected in the imaginative writing of the time, especially in poetry. It is interesting to note how much of the verse of so contemplative a poet as Wordsworth was affected or directly called forth by the Napoleonic Wars, and previously by the French Revolution. Later in France, Germany, and Italy, and still later in Russia, popular revolutions created or revivified national literatures.

By way of contrast it is interesting also to note that English fiction during the whole century was unperturbed, yielding scarcely an echo to these exciting Continental tumults. In their peaceful insulation the novelists, from Jane Austen to Thomas Hardy, were oblivious to all outward disturbances. England had, for her island domain at least, achieved the peace and freedom which are essential to the quiet expansion of culture.

After the Revolution of 1688 England steadily

advanced in the development of her empire abroad and, at the same time, of free institutions at home; and to both is due the superiority of English to Continental fiction. The sense of national greatness and that of personal liberty and security inspired and determined the aim and character of this fiction. These conditions provided a constantly increasing audience for literature in books and periodicals.

Thus we account for the quiet atmosphere of English fiction since Fielding—almost provincially quiet if we exclude historical romances. It has been left to historians and poets to celebrate martial triumphs—Blenheim, Waterloo, Balaklava, and the rest, and even lately Watson and Kipling have kindled sparks from Bellona's anvil. This kind of heroism, in the reproduction of which the measure of verse has always so aptly responded to that of the march, has never strongly moved the English novelist, not simply because he was writing prose, but because he preferred to portray struggles, excitements, and enthusiasms of another character—such as grew out of the lives about him, open to his observation and appealing to his sympathy and to his sense of humor. Thomas Hardy, in his recent elaborate epic drama, shows this lingering preference, unable to cast aside the habit which he had acquired as a novelist. The main current of English fiction has been domestic and social, bound up with the lives of the people and little concerned with martial pomp and circumstance.

The mildness of our season in literature seems, then, not so new a thing, after all. We cannot fairly say that it is an autumnal mildness, a sign of decadence, since it was with us in the spring and summer; indeed, for all we know, it is still the spring-time, or the opening summer, of a bountiful era. Any forebodings we may indulge must have their ground in the assumption that civilization itself is a movement whose ultimate issue is decay.

It is commonly held that at least every particular cycle of the movement must have this mortal issue, just as surely in the career of a race as in that of an individual. The decline of every ancient civilization is adduced as a convincing demonstration of this position. But is it convincing? Have we not already reached a point where, in this respect, history can no longer be said to repeat itself?

It is not so very long since astronomers regarded it as a foregone conclusion that the universe was, as a whole, doomed to dissolution at the end of some "grand cycle." But new systems are forever emerging in the depths of space, and our conviction of a final and total cataclysm is shaken. So it is possible that our modern civilization may last as long as this planet is habitable. The peoples of the earth no longer confront any inevitable bankruptcy of material resources; on the contrary, as Professor Patten has recently shown, they are assured a con-stantly increasing surplus, whereas up to a com-paratively recent date they faced a deficit. Older nations were, moreover, embroiled in perpetual wars, the most efficient of them all being finally supplanted by more virile Northern races.

The bright manifesto of progress, at the beginning of the twentieth century, promises the abolition of poverty and the early advent of peace among those nations which no longer suffer from barbaric conditions such as impede the development of Russia. There is now no reasonable ground for the final decadence of any race save through its spiritual degeneration. This is the vital point. A people may enjoy the greatest possible physical comfort and sanity, with civil liberty, perfect administrative efficiency, irreproachable morality, and even the most strenuous altruism, and it may be as sane mentally as we are supposing it to be physically; but, while it would be safe from corruption, if all this efficiency has been gained at the expense of creative power, such a people has paid too high a price for the benefits of progress. Lacking spiritual humor, insight, and sympathy, it could have no essential greatness in its life or in its literature.

If our modern civilization cannot meet this challenge, then Christendom is a meaningless term.

We have to consider not simply or mainly the achievements of progress, but the more essential values disclosed in the course of human evolution.

We cannot doubt the efficiency of modern institutions, and it is hardly possible for us to conceive the greater perfectibility yet to be attained, along the lines already developed, by the co-operation of civilized nations. But questions arise quite independent of such attainments, and not concerning goals to be reached but rather sources, in the native and original powers of the human spirit. The humanities are not achievements. The hopeful signs in plain evidence on a superficial view—the greater freedom and security of the individual, the better sanitation, the better educational outlook, the ameliorated conditions of workers, old and young, the advance in private and public morality, the growth of the sentiment in favor of military and naval disarmament—all these are in themselves only improvements, our manifest gains in bargains we have been all along making with destiny. They do not relieve our solicitude as to values far transcending such betterments. Almost generally the assumption prevails that genius, originality of character, the picturesqueness of life, and the illusions of faith have been broken up, if not destroyed, by the corrosive analyses of science, by an aggressive and all-absorbing commercial spirit, and by the weight and complexity of organization in every department of activity.

Let us clearly distinguish between the values gained through our experience and those which spring from creative evolution—that is, from native powers, the most distinctive of which is the imagination, "the vision and the faculty divine." We cannot develop imaginative power or imaginative sensibility through a progressive experience as, through that experience, we develop wisdom in the adaptation of means to ends, thus acquiring skill and efficiency. This native power has not progress, but evolution—such as goes on in the natural world, with transmutation of the forms disclosed at successive stages of the genetic procedure. Human progress, as indicated in its results, is empirical, the sum of effort and experimentation, following a logical process of thought. The evolution of genius, in life, literature, and art, discloses effects that are spontaneous, inevitable, unpremeditated, and therefore not precalculable—births, not fashioned products. Such effects are the genesis of language, the creation of myth and of mythological personages, singing, dancing, the birth of the epic, of the drama, of architecture, sculpture, and painting, and of the modern art of fiction.

This is but a partial summary. Passing from art to life itself, the genetic procedure of the evolution is more profoundly interesting and significant, and its effects, as distinguished from those achieved in the course of human progress, far more wonderful, though more evanescent. In the earliest period, before the exploitation of the world by human ingenuity and artifice, genius had the whole field to itself; art and nature were inseparably blended in a life not yet sharply detached from the physical world. The flowers of that human garden passed away with their blooming, and we can only conjecture, from later evidences, how soon such Eden as there may have been was despoiled by the institutional tyrannies of kingcraft and priestcraft which presided over what was then styled progress; we only dimly glimpse those ancient festivals—their lights and shadows—and can only imagine the purple hues of the glowing picture, the plaintive notes of the choral song. But then, as during the whole long period of the old aristocratic *régime*, there *was* the festival, with its choral and picturesque accompaniments; there was, within poignant limitations, the spontaneous up-springing of the joys of life, domestic and social and under gracious skies—and even the slave had the freedom of his dreams, if he might only dream of Elysian fields beyond. These native delights are indefinable, but they are fruits of the creative life, as are human romance, heroism, and enthusiasm. In the ancient world we see them at their best in Hellas, where the passing æsthetic excellence in life became fixed in enduring shapes of beauty. The Hellenic type of man was itself an emergence in this creative evolution: it was unattainable as a result of progress. The shaping genius is manifest in the race before it can emerge in individual or collective life or in the work of the artist.

As we contemplate this side of human life, finding it difficult to definitely express the traits of it which are so indefinable, inevitably and helpfully the words of the Master present themselves to our minds, free from dogmatic translation and ecclesiastic obscuration. We behold, in spiritual intuition, the things revealed to babes and hidden from worldly wisdom and phariseeism—the humors, insouciances, and unmoralities, the blended dove-and-serpent type of life.

In this field, too, are the passions, good or evil, as we call them, just as we distinguish between what is benevolent and what is malsaine in the physical world. They are the chief motor-powers in the earthly expression of the creative life, and their conflict is its drama.

But what most profoundly impresses us is the mystery of personality itself — the being of men, women, and children as distinct from life's busyness —the something which art embodies, and which the writer of fiction creates but cannot describe.


Specialization, which in progressive experience means improved efficiency, in evolution means new forms of life. Here we confront the question as to gains and losses. But in every form the question takes, it is as if we asked: Is it better to be the planet or the star? At every stage of universal evolution there seems to be a surrender of power for some special excellence. We can estimate the gains, but we have no arithmetic subtle enough to calculate the losses. Some kind of psychical essences may inhabit the stars, from whom we are descended and who were sponsors at our aboriginal christening.

How should we know? The Angel of the Sun is silent.

But we do know that the emergence of organic and, sequently, of human life upon the earth was permitted only after the planet had given up a large measure of its heat and all of its self-radiance and had established an extremely modest temperament. Structural strength seems to be gained at the loss of much of that creative power which resides in plastic forms. In all this diminution and descent there is apparent a normal decadence, through which the cosmic order is permitted to exist and to enter into its wonderful heritage of varied beauty.

The values thus permitted in the course of human evolution are those we most prize, and, even if we were able to count the cost, it is not likely that we would wish to reverse our course, any more than we would regret the abjectness of the planet or desire to return to a sexless kingdom of unicellular organisms which was abandoned on pain of mortality.

We cheerfully share in the descents, which alone are visible, having faith in the ascension of life, which is hidden from us, willingly giving ourselves up to the beneficent stream, though the paths by which its fountains are replenished are invisible.

Creative power is not really lost in the apparent surrenders we have made in the evolutionary procedure; it has only taken upon itself new veils, appearing thus ever again in fresher charm and more gracious offices.

Having seen what permission is given to new and more abundant life in a natural and normal descent, we may more easily comprehend the permissive conditions which our physical, mental, and moral progress has afforded for such life and for imaginative creaton in art and literature.

This progress at its root—that is, as growing out of the emergence of rational consciousness, the ground of arbitrary volition and selection—is itself evolutionary, and we should also so consider it in its totality if we could view it as a completed cycle; but its procedure is, at every point of its departure from native and instinctive processes, so apparently contradictory to natural evolution that, because of our inability to find the means of reconciliation between it and nature, we must be content to follow the lines of its divergence. An immense advantage was gained through the specialization which made man an empiricist, enabling him to devise means for the accomplishment in a brief period of what, without his experimental intervention, Nature would take ages to bring about—of what indeed for the most part would never have come within the scope of natural operation. Nature simply went on in her fixed circle, but in doing so she was made to effect man's deliberate purposes, he only putting the wisely chosen element or machine in her path. Most of man's work is done for him in this way by natural forces. By his dependence upon reasoning processes his native instinct was veiled, persisting in his passions and taking new forms in his æsthetic faculty and sensibility and in all the creative processes of his genius in life and art.

Progress, even under the old aristocratic *régime*, brought about, for the few, conditions of wealth, luxury, and culture, which favored the manifestations of genius, to a higher degree and with more eminent results, many academic critics maintain, than is possible in a democratic society. To us it seems that the progress of the last century, so wonderful because of the general advance in popular freedom and general education, has especially afforded permissive conditions for new species in the creative evolution of life and literature. We are not disappointed because there are no giants in these days. The deeper sensibility calls for finer forms and has no regret that so much of pomp and majesty has passed away. Imagination in the best of our literature meets our life on even terms and has no advantage in its creations over the spontaneous outgrowths of that life, save in its greater freedom of selection; it has no separate ideals, no discrete material for the texture of its living pictures and characterizations, no unlike passions in its drama, no diverse atmosphere. Its temperament, like that of our life, is modulated. It is natural in that it repudiates gloss and artifice. This imagination has made Science something more than a classification of phenomena by giving it a pregnant co-ordination, so that it is a fertile field of wonders which, to our modern sensibility, are more interesting as well as more satisfactory, in poetic values, than ancient myths or mediæval legends.

Literature, following the same lines, rejecting the unreal, has become homely of feature, with home-like sympathies, graces, and charms, and at the same time more subtle and wonderful in its disclosure of the deep truths of life than it ever was in its detachment from life or in its reflection of a life which had not found its true centre in a spiritual harmony and was therefore itself untrue, wearing all sorts of illusive or monstrous disguises.

On the structural side creative life and literature have gained from the ingenuity and adaptive wisdom acquired in progressive human experience; while a pervading reasonableness is their pellucid atmosphere. Choice, control, and reflection enter as almost consciously determinant elements in this cosmic order; old violences are subdued and elemental passions tempered. Our sensibility revolts from the volcanic and the gigantesque. By our effort or through wisdom gained by our experience we can neither bring into being nor destroy any of the primary elements of nature or of human nature with which we deal and which deal with us. In the garden which we tend, every living thing springs up spontaneously, with its proper shape, fragrance, and flavor, responsive to a sensibility equally native and spontaneous, but both the garden and our sensibility answer to our tillage and culture.

# CHAPTER IV

## REACTION OF GENIUS UPON THE WORLD

W E were showing how evolution and progress played into each other's hands, which
is natural, seeing that progress, at its root
and at every point of its course which marks a
fresh beginning, is itself evolutionary.

Thus we may consider democracy as an institutional development, in different degrees of efficiency
at different periods of human experience. That is
its progress. But when we regard it in its origin and
in its transformations at critical epochs, we find
that we must refer it to impulses of the human
spirit which transcend experimentation and belong
to our creative life. That is its evolution. Seen
thus in its beginnings, its new births, we co-ordinate
it with those other creative manifestations through
which the human spirit has been emancipated. So
language in its genesis is of evolution and continues
to be genetic in the writer's or speaker's expression
when that expression is a fresh embodiment of imaginative thought or feeling, appealing to imaginative
sensibility; but simply as an instrument of com-

munication for ordinary uses it is an indispensable factor in progress. Thought itself arises independently of our conscious volition, is genetic, as is our first knowledge, and in original device and invention it is creative; but, as adaptive through obvious means to definitely conceived ends, it merely subserves the utility of progress. Habit is originally the investment of creative desire, but, as a habiliment arbitrarily assumed, it becomes a fashion or a convention. Crystallization supervenes when life is reduced to its lowest terms, and this is broken up by a creative transformation, which is evolutionary, awaiting only the permissive conditions. Choice is originally instinctive selection, the immediate and spontaneous dilection of the creative and creatively shaping imagination; but when it becomes consciously arbitrary, as in all experimentation, the creative determination is no longer apparent, being at least held in abeyance, and the successes thus achieved, after however many failures, make for the efficiency which registers human progress as distinguished from the evolution of humanity.

All the critical epochs of progress, in so far as they are renascences of the human spirit, are evolutionary. The greatest of these renascences in history was Christianity, which had the divine felicity of embodiment in a singular human personality, resuming all the powers of a creative life—powers distinctive to a kingdom of never-ceasing renascence, subject to no confinement, and transcending all sacred enclosures and rituals. This personality becomes thus the Evangel of genius, which pays conventional tribute and is yet free, and resumes at once the powers of childhood and the most subtile wisdom.

Genius is common to humanity, but those of her children who most cherish her, choosing the good part, may well heed many a gospel reminder—especially those which call attention to the superior wisdom, in some respects, of the children of the world to that of the children of light, and which enjoin friendship with those who build more lasting earthly habitations—lessons to which Tolstoy paid so much regard in his art and so little in his philosophy. The meek would hardly inherit the earth save as they combine the wisdom of serpents with the harmlessness of doves. To teach the necessity of a firm foundation for a durable edifice and of a fertile soil to a fruitful harvest savors even of pragmatism. The plasticity of genius, like that of faith, is the ground of all miracle, but structural strength is essential to firm consistency of character and work.

Ingenuity as a trait of genius means something more than it means even in the most exquisite daedalian artifice; it involves the kind of imaginative co-ordination which in the thought of Newton identified the falling of an apple with cosmic gravitation — the kind which has prompted those inventions that have transformed modern economies. It is implied in the rhythm of sculpture, as in that of music and poetry, and in the composition of a great painting.

Progress owes more to genius than genius does to progress  Creative imagination gave spectrum analysis to science, and a like ingenuity prompted the application of its principle to the Bessemer process in the manufacture of steel.  In the mind of Clerk-Maxwell this ingenuity anticipated and stimulated those experiments which prepared the way for the complex functions of electricity in modern industries, just as in the mind of Laplace it had originated the masterly analysis which laid the foundations of the mathematical sciences of heat, electricity, and magnetism; in the minds of Röntgen, Thompson, Ramsay, and Rutherford it has disclosed a new world of radiant phenomena; and what it has prompted in other departments of chemistry for commercial uses Professor Duncan has abundantly demonstrated.  The "New Knowledge" finds its leading clues, even in philosophy, in these disclosures of evolutionary processes by evolutionary insight. It is genetic, as the first knowledge was, only it sees in the light what it first felt toward in the dark.

In fiction the author deals altogether with evolutionary processes and features in his portrayal of human nature, as manifestly he must in such portrayal of nature as may come within the scope of his art.  The new truths disclosed to him, which he embodies in living individual characters and weaves into the social texture he creates, involve on his part, though through a different method, a more flexile and varied ingenuity, in insight and invention, than that which distinguishes the masters in science and philosophy or artists in other fields. Indeed, he combines all these masteries, though not in just the same forms of analysis or synthesis. His imagination appeals directly to the intellectual sensibility as that of the great master in science or philosophy does; but it also appeals directly to the emotional sensibility in a way that the scientific and philosophic imagination does not. The sculptor and painter and architect appeal to æsthetic sensibility through the eye, as the musician does through the ear. The novelist is not subject to these limitations—the whole heart and mind of the reader are directly responsive to his.

The sculptor for the durability of his work seizes upon and masters an alien material at once resistant and plastic to his hand, and the beholder of the finished statue or statuary group at once detects a fault of form or of rhythmic harmony. The obligations of the art are as obvious as they are rigid. This is the case also in music and poetry. In fiction there is relaxation and free play as to both theme and method, and, in the judgment of it, a more recondite appreciation is demanded, unaided by the eye or ear. The writer more easily deceives himself and others as to the values of his work on the structural side. It is as essential to him as it is to the sculptor that there should be action and reaction in his relation to his material, though that material is not the hard marble. Tension is as necessary to his imaginative creation as it is to that of the poet, though it is not released in metrical forms.

Genius, in this field, may and often does fail of mastery because of the very freedom of its realm and the facility of its medium—that is, of words,—and if it also has a loose hold upon its material, its energy is dissipated, and there can be no consistency of structure. It is as if growth were arrested in infancy. In such cases genius has no vertebrate strength, no seizure upon the world, no nutriment but "the milk of paradise." In the imaginative literature it produces we see only the fluent traits of childhood—infantile grace, quaintness, and *naïveté*. It is spontaneous, genuine, and, within its limitations, charming and wonderful, having the positive quality which more than any other is the essential characteristic of genius, but no firm embodiment, no lasting habitation. We find its counterpart in the lives of Christians who seclude themselves from the world and become Quietists or Non-resistants.

Genius in this arrested development is most often overcome by the world through the perversions of education or of individual and social experience. On the contrary, it should overcome the world, by appetite and seizure. Else, even if it escapes suppression and passes into its second stage—that of assimilation—instead of assimilating its proper material for its own nutrition and expansion it becomes simply imitative, and lacking root and tension of its own, is again arrested within the limitations of an adopted fashion.

The writer whose genius is persistent passes through these two stages we have indicated, but with a different attitude toward the world it is given him to master. In him the creative imagination is from the first, even in its plastic beginnings, a craving appetite, taking its kingdom with violence. In its nurture such is the absorption and tension that silence marks its course, such expression as there is in this period being incidental. It is well if the period of nutrition is prolonged, as indeed it is sure to be, according to the scope and destiny of the individual genius. The world seems to exist for the reaction upon it of such an imagination as Shakespeare's—the robber of other men's stores and of all the treasuries of nature and humanity.

For here too there is assimilation—not through adoptive imitation—and with it a response to leading notes, but the master finds in due time his own centre, his individual note. He is not of the world, though it is his heritage. Not one of the objects of human pursuit or of human progress is an object of his attainment, though of humanity itself every passion, every hope and fear, every feature of its complex drama, is an intimate concern of his art and enters into its structure. Heroism, romance, faith, as elements of our common human nature, are at his command for enchantment and illumination, while the sadness and trouble of the world, the faultfulness of men and women, and the inevitable dooms of fate furnish only too readily the glooms and shadows of his drama. Provided he creates characters of living men and women and discloses the real truth and meaning of their lives, nothing which concerns these lives—religious feeling, affection, institutional conditions, social impulses, good and evil passions, or the stress and pain of the everlasting human conflict—is forbidden him. His imagination seizes upon this living material which is subject to his selection, in the line of his individual appetite; and in this line all his faculties and sensibilities are eagerly engaged. This is his special culture.

Thus Dickens devoured his England. Thus Hewlett has preyed upon his Italy. Other writers accumulate facts and give us information, or collect data which they use in pleading special causes. The novelist has no such purposes, no concern apart from his creative representation of life, and in so far as he attempts anything beyond this, however fine or sympathetic his intention, his creative power is held in abeyance. The characterization in Mrs. Gaskell's *Mary Barton* is for this reason far inferior to that in her *Cranford.*

No novelist of our time has to such an extent assimilated the culture of the modern world as Mrs. Humphry Ward, and none has made a wiser use of it for the purposes of her art. She is the greatest institutional novelist in the whole range of English fiction. But, however complex the social background of any of her more important recent novels, she has done full justice to it without loss of creative power in characterization or dramatic representation. Perhaps no better example could be found of the effective use by an adept novelist of present social and political conditions in England than is furnished in the early chapters of *The Testing of Diana Mallory*. The new order of things comes well to the front in Tallyn Hall, where Diana, who has just returned from India to an England she has not seen since infancy, participates in her first social function. Her pride is in the empire and the army; but the contest in which she stands at bay, so finely and truly portrayed in every feature of it, is not allowed to possess the reader for its own issues, but only to concentrate his interest upon the girl, upon her frank, resistant spirit, in a situation which we prophetically discern as pathetic, even while the elements which make it so are yet unknown to us, veiled in the mystery which has surrounded her from birth. All the circumstances of this brilliantly pictured social party in Tallyn Hall, every detail — even the ugly frescos representing the progress of the Iron Trade—every character introduced, derive their significance to the reader from their relation to Diana Mallory.

But for this absorbing dramatic prepossession, how interesting all the features which compose the background would be in themselves! As it is, the impression abides with us, a conciliating satisfaction on its own account. How many world-pictures in Mrs. Ward's previous fiction do we treasure in our memories, after the individual human dramas associated with them have had their day with us! How many, too, from Meredith's and Hardy's! Sir Gilbert Parker's novel, *The Weavers*, is full of them, so thoroughly had its author mastered his Egypt, and so readily does his imagination evoke not only the vivid Oriental picture, but the wonderful impressions of that life in which the West meets the East. All this we shall treasure when even so great a personality as he has created for us in David shall be forgotten, though in reading the novel we are never permitted to forget him, however fascinating the background.

In some creations of the imagination the human drama is so absorbing that striking individual character and the interest of the situation seem sufficient. This is especially so with that kind of fiction which, as in the case of Dickens, most nearly resembles modern stage representations. Humor is dissipated by the distractions of an elaborate background. Comedy is confined within the limits of the contemporaneous and familiar scene. The flavor of the story of provincial life and character will not bear the admixture of anything foreign to itself. Romance, on the other hand, has always thrived on strange elements, being by nature as nomadic as the gypsy or troubadour. Intellectual curiosity is in this respect most nearly allied to romance, and, as it seeks new disclosures in science, so, in all the higher forms of entertainment, it craves new knowledge of the world and of humanity. The interest of the modern novel depends ever more and more upon the writer's power to meet and satisfy this higher curiosity, to create and multiply new forms of intellectual excitement, and just in the degree of the story's intension and of the writer's mastery of subjective psychical phenomena, is there the need of extension of the world affiliations with the human drama.

Thus the modern sensibility, which is more and more a feeling of the mind, veiling elemental passion, grows tolerant of the elaborate background, even at the sacrifice of striking character and of sensational emotion, provided it is not a contrived background, but a creation of the imagination. We have at least one instance—in Hichens's *The Garden of Allah*—where the writer's imagination is exhausted in what might be called the characterization of the background, a complex portraiture of the desert, with a subsidiary story that serves only as its reflex, the man and the woman chosen for this purpose representing the human sensibility which determines the impressions conveyed. That such a novel should prove commercially successful shows to what an extent the imaginative sensibility of readers has been developed—also the avidity of its craving for those new disclosures which genius makes through its mastery of world-material as well as of mind-material.

Neither of *The Garden of Allah* nor of Mr. Hichens's more recent novel, *Barbary Sheep*, its natural successor, has the reader cause for complaint because of any lack of dramatic satisfaction, though it is the Desert that is dramatized and characterized — the Desert in its contacts with the human soul. In the appeal which the author makes to the higher, or psychical, curiosity, he stands at the opposite extreme, in the evolution of the imagination, to the old-fashioned playwright and story-teller. His work is thus a remarkable illustration of the vast departure of our fiction from its earliest appeal to a crude sensibility, which found complete, but narrow, satisfaction in stirring narrative and thrilling dramatic situations.

The scheme of the novel has widened with the desire for new knowledge of the real world without us and within us—not information, or logical deductions therefrom, but interpretation, illumination. It is a kind of curiosity which cannot be trifled with by any of the old tricks. The demand upon the writer of fiction has grown more exacting, if we consider only his theme, without any reference to his art of expression. He must have hunger and thirst for reality, the invention that finds it, the ingenuity which is the insight of genius in the great discovery.

# CHAPTER V

## THE DEPARTURE FROM THE VICTORIAN ERA

WE have had so much to say about the "new literature" that we might very well be challenged to give some positive definition of it, and to show wherein it is new and what evolutionary advantage or value is disclosed in the variation.

The new literature is not our discovery. Current criticism has not failed to recognize and discerningly appreciate its values. In these pages we have participated in that criticism, and, we confess, with much zest, as well as with a natural pride, because it is in periodicals that this new literature has had its amplest opportunity and representation, so that magazine readers are, above all others, best prepared for an intelligent comprehension of its novel flavors, having so abundantly partaken of the fresh vintage.

Otherwise we should despair of any adequate characterization of that kind of imaginative creation which—as we have claimed—belongs distinctively to our own time. The full presentment has been, for a large number of readers, actually made, and in their minds exists the background necessary to an intelligible critical or interpretative comment. It would be impossible to show what is the new quality of imaginative writing in such authors as Conrad, Hewlett, Hichens, Kenneth Grahame, or Alfred Ollivant to readers unacquainted with their creations; but no one can have read a single one of their works without a vivid sense of something so novel as to be unprecedented. The very mention of their names suggests a quality which, for what it is in itself, no critic can define, but which goes far to illuminate the distinction which we wish to emphasize.

These are English names; but while in America the distinction belongs mainly to short stories, it is apparent also in the work of some of our recent and contemporary novelists—those who, like Henry James, William Dean Howells, Henry Harland, Owen Wister, Edith Wharton, Margaret Deland, and Mary Austin, have departed from the traditions of the Victorian era. It is in the short stories of the last ten years that this departure is most evident and that distinctively new features in our imaginative literature—so new as to be unprecedented—are most clearly manifest. The novelists we have named have illustrated this new literature chiefly in short stories, while it is in these alone that other writers have been eminent from this point of view—Georg Schock, Muriel Campbell Dyar, Jennette Lee, Margaret Cameron, Forrest Crissey, Elmore Elliot Peake, James Branch Cabell, Justus Miles Forman, Norman Duncan, and, notably, Grace Ellery Channing.

Enlarging the compass of our retrospect so as to cover the last quarter of a century of English and American fiction, we have a fairer representation of the new literature in its inception. This period would include the mature work of Henry James, whose extreme modernity is unquestioned; *A Modern Instance* and *The Rise of Silas Lapham* by Howells, whose spirit and aim in fiction as well as his critical view of its proper scope and method give him the position of a leader in this new path; the most important novels of Mrs. Humphry Ward, in the texture of which, though more than any other contemporary writer she maintains the continuity of culture from the Victorian era to our own, she has advanced *per saltum* into a field not cultivated even by George Eliot; the fiction of Mary Wilkins, after her native genius had taken on form and structure; Sarah Orne Jewett's rural sketches; Kipling's short stories, and the best work of Mark Twain.

This period reaches back far enough to include characteristic examples of the work of two writers—Thomas Hardy and George Meredith—who came into their own, indeed, in the Victorian era, but were wholly distinct from the group to which Thackeray, Dickens, Reade, and George Eliot belonged. They were prophets of a coming literature, whose writers call them masters—Meredith for his appeal to the intellectual sensibility, while Hardy's work has been more eminently representative of the new creative faculty than that of his successors.

# THE DEPARTURE FROM THE VICTORIAN ERA

To have passed beyond these writers into new fields is not to have surpassed them. Such an advance has been made, but we are not claiming for the fresh variations of our present literature, however novel or unprecedented, any superior eminence. Greatness is possible in the future, as it has been in the past, through some surprising emergence of individual genius, but it will be greatness of a new order, not having the insignia of what was accounted greatness in any previous time. The writers who hold the advance in our generation are not greater than their predecessors, but they prosper through their appeal to an advanced sensibility.

## CHAPTER VI

### CHANGES IN HUMAN NATURE

NO notion is more obstinately maintained than that human nature is the same in all ages. "Essentially the same," the phrase usually runs, thus leading on to a particularly infertile ontological speculation. We do not know what anything essentially is—what the "thing in itself" is—but only phenomena, and only such phenomena as are realized for us within the range of our perception, the scope of which science has considerably enlarged. It is only through changes in things without us or in ourselves that we know at all, that we have consciousness.

The idea of sameness does not belong to the content of any real knowledge of ours, and occurs to us only after or along with our sense of some difference or change, as a complement or reflex, due to a very useful and quite indispensable mental habit, but for which any generalization would be impossible, or even the idea of personal identity, or such a process as memory. But inevitable and important as this habit is—as important as the attraction of gravitation is in the universe,—the bond of all our diverse expanse of knowledge, it is and must forever remain something wholly of the mind, not a constituent element of our perception of what is going on without us or within us. The idea of sameness is, then, a notion, in a negative way agreeable and satisfactory when we reflect upon its constitutional value —as when we reflect upon that of gravitation—but not particularly or really interesting. It is the diversity and expansion which engage in a positive way our eager curiosity and interest.

We note this element of positive pleasure and excitement in scientific pursuits. The investigator, while he is duly grateful for his ability to classify phenomena, and especially for that power of coordination which is distinctive of the scientific imagination, does not rest in his generalizations, but goes on seeking new diversities and variations which disclose evolution, thus adding to the stock of real knowledge, which is a sure possession, and from time to time he finds that some of the generalizations which seemed sure and sufficient have to be abandoned, however serviceable they may have been temporarily.

The story of electricity illustrates our point. This force was always as important physically and physiologically as it is to-day; but the ancients knew nothing of it except as apparent in the amber which gave it its name. Only within about a century and a half was it identified with its most common and at the same time most striking physical manifestation—the lightning. In general it was a continuous current, everywhere flowing, but unknown because unbroken. In the course of scientific experimentation the current was broken, was discriminated as positive and negative; and, following it by the flashes of its brokenness, we have now a voluminous record of real knowledge concerning it and a special system of mathematics whereby we have measured what we had so compoundly divided. Its co-ordination with light, heat, and magnetism, intimating a beautiful harmony, was an inevitable consequence of disclosures resulting from a careful study of the phenomena of these forces and of their common mathematics; but the likeness is not so really interesting to us as the specialization, the lines of which, in infinite variations, we are still following with ever-increasing zest.

The student of the cell knows how complete a mask, which even the microscope cannot penetrate, identity is—or at least what seems absolute identity; but he knows also how quickly germination unmasks the variant life.

Herbert Spencer's first proposition concerning evolution—that it is the development of the heterogeneous from the homogeneous—is significant. The heterogeneity is evident enough, but the primary homogeneity is merely a notion. Sameness, or what is mentally presumed to be sameness, is, in this aboriginal case, an immense mask, which no human wisdom can penetrate, and we have to substitute for it Mutability itself as primary—the creative determination toward infinite specialization. Universal homogeneity, as a reality, is inconceivable.

Could anything be duller than history written with a view to prove or illustrate the persistent uniformity of human nature? We know, indeed, that some things are normally common to all men in their physical and mental constitution; and if we could put ourselves back to that remote period when humanity had not risen above the plane of the animal, or above the mentality incident to his actions and passions on such a plane, when what seemed his possibilities could be predicated, as in the case of other animals, from his physical structure, including his brain—if there ever was such a period, however brief,—we might be impressed by a sense of uniformity, in a general way corresponding to our sense of uniformity in Nature. It would not be a situation pleasant to contemplate, since it must have been one in which the comparative inferiority of the human species would be strikingly manifest. In such sameness of human nature as would thus be presented we should confront a mask hiding everything which we count distinctive of humanity.

Our historical researches do not enable us to even approach such a period, but they carry us back far enough to disclose a humanity so intimately blended with Nature that we still confront an impenetrable mask, hiding man's proper destiny as completely as the barren primeval earth withheld from possible prevision her future investiture of life and beauty.

This primitive period endured the longest and was the most persistent in stability of any in human history, having only a fragmentary record, since there was so little in it worthy of any record. So lacking in diversity, it could not minister to our intellectual diversion. The student whose regard is most closely confined to a remote view of humanity is naturally disposed to insist upon the everlasting sameness of human nature, not merely in its constituent elements, but in its motives, impulses, and sense of life. We are not surprised, therefore, that so eminent an archæologist as Flinders Petrie should lay such stress upon this view as he does in his *Janus in Modern Life*, which in every other way is most pertinently and intensely modern.

The moment man transcended the scope of physical action and passion, the mentality incident to these, and an exclusive regard for primary family and social relations consequent upon them — the moment of his psychical awakening, when his imagination entered its distinctive realm, and creatively projected its embodiments, no longer confined to those primitive choric, lyric, and dramatic manifestations in which the physical body is an indispensable participant—that moment of escape from the chrysalis of humanity marked the commencement of a series of marvellous changes which were transformations of human nature itself. This is the course of evolution—on the lower and primary plane long periods with few and almost imperceptible variations; on the higher, a more and more rapid succession of distinct epochs with ever-increasing variations, until it is convincingly apparent that man, in the accomplishment of his proper destiny, is of all beings the most mutable.

The field of his mutability is the widest, in part because, as, having choice, he is the master of materials and of limitless artifice through the immense range of artificial selection, and, as having a progressively complex consciousness, he is the one earthly spectator of the course of things and events in the world outside of him and of human phenomena; but chiefly because of his psychical faculty and sensibility, as having creative imagination, the determinant of his faith, his art, his literature, his philosophy—all of his life that gives him distinction and that makes his human history interesting.

Now the mutations in the psychical world correspond to those in Nature in that they are genetic, or creative, transformations; that is, evolutionary, as distinguished from the changes that occur in progressive experience, due to arbitrary selection, to conscious adaptation of means to ends. They are necessary to explain why man has that intermediary wisdom by which he is the singular artificer, the builder of civilizations, for of what worth are all his devices without this psychical evolution? But for this evolution all his discourse of reason would be a barren and inexplicable waste.

But, as the master artificer, he has such power to promote psychical changes in himself as he has to affect natural processes, through his arbitrary selection. Owing to what he has fashioned, to the artificial elements of his civilization, the psychical transformations have had even a more rapid succession. His freedom of choice saves him from confinement to the fixed circles in which Nature moves, and there is no possible mathematical calculation of any critical moment marking his ascensions or declinations; while his power to determine to so great an extent his own environment is a new acceleration of his progress, affording fresh permissive conditions of his psychical evolution. Every vantage gained for individual liberty through institutional advance, inspired by new awakenings of the human spirit, has multiplied these permutations.

The radical changes in human nature belong to the psychical field, but we must include in our consideration not only what the creative imagination has been in science, art, literature, faith, and philosophy, but what it has been in life, independently of these. It is true that we can have no idea of any past age, in this respect, as real as that we have of our own, because the phenomena are so evanescent and can only be indirectly suggested by accessible records, though more adequately by literature than in any other way. If these phenomena could be reproduced for us in their reality, the great civilizations of the past would disclose more delicate graces and beauties of social intercourse than can be divined by the archæologist or the historian. The Homeric poems incidentally give us glimpses of such qualities in the life to which these old epics belong, and, as truly as these, due to the creative imagination, shaping the spiritual features of that life.

There were as good codes of morality, indicating as much regard for the obvious virtues, six thousand years ago as we have to-day; but blended with this morality in human action were positive excellences, independent of formal injunction, making up the full embodiment of such ideals as were possible. It is in this spiritual physiognomy—which we call, in the largest sense, Manners—that the conduct of human life has been undergoing marvellous changes during two hundred generations; and these transformations have, in every stage of the evolution, been reflected in art and literature—in all the monuments of creative imagination—rather than in institutional forms and conventions, which would forever remain the same, in obstinate stability, but for the psychical renewals of the whole fabric of life, a good part of them, indeed, being retained from age to age because of their permanent formal value. If we could have as clear and full view of the old times as of our own, we should see that in every distinctive aspect of human life the distinction is to be accounted for by the creatively shaping imagination which determines man's psychical destiny in its limitless range of transmutations.

Just here we confidently meet Flinders Petrie's assertion that "the nature of mind is unchanged, its motives, its feelings, its sense of life; only in knowledge and the applications of it do we differ from the earliest civilization that we can trace. . . . The mind is the same, only the stock-in-trade of it has increased." It is surprising to find such a view expressed by an author who admits and lays stress upon an evolution in mind corresponding to that in Nature. Knowledge is not simply cumulative—an ever-increasing "stock-in-trade"—unless we limit it to mere information; it has evolutionary variations in which the creative imagination is not only participant but determinant.

The fund of information is cumulative, and may be transmitted from generation to generation. But a new "sense of life," or of the world, can originate only with some renascence of sensibility itself. New knowledge, in this sense of it, is possible only as man psychically experiences new birth. In some of its features, advanced civilization involves merely modification of conditions and methods; in other and distinctive aspects it is a continuous creation, involving renewals of human nature.

The first projections of the imagination in religion and art, simply as projections, are significant of a mighty transformation by which man created something, beyond himself and beyond the world next to him, in what we call mythology. Still retaining the old method of physical expression, through the dance and the use of nature-symbols, his crude accompanying lyric leaped to overtones which he seemed to overhear and which suggested a transcendent kinship. The myth was born, and a way was disclosed leading humanity out of its primitive naturalism. The ritual was continued, but was radically modified; the story of the god was interjected, giving it a new meaning, attractive enough to arrest the processional for its hearing. In poetry and in the plastic arts there was a like projection of the imagination, concentrating upon the new and lofty theme. The glory of the Hellenic civilization became possible to men who loved the sea, who were not rooted in the soil nor slavishly held by the old naturalistic bond, and who may be said to have projected themselves and their life to the same heights their art and their faith inhabited, breaking away from agricultural isolation and becoming the builders of cities. Human instincts were psychically illuminated and uplifted, permitting a nobler development of domestic affection, of friendship, of romantic love, of general social intercourse, and of a patriotism freed from tribal limitation and nourishing the desire for civic freedom —at least for a select body of citizens.

If we pass abruptly from this pagan civilization, the most excellent of antiquity, to that which flourished in the cities of Italy after the revival of learning—if we pass from Sophocles and Phidias to Dante and Michelangelo—we find the same projectiveness of the imagination, a more elaborate pageantry, the mute participation of the multitude, but, beneath and in all this spectacle, we discern a new human nature, not only as manifest in the creations of art and in psychical sensibility, but also in impulses, motives, and the sense of life, responsive to a loftier and deeply heart-searching theme.

Passing from Dante to Wordsworth, the psychical transformation is still more wonderful, and includes a large body of the English - speaking people who have achieved individual freedom of selection and interpretation.

In these long leaps, from age to age, the radical changes in human nature become evident at a glance and without laborious discrimination. But we are living in a time when a decade stands for an epoch in psychical evolution. There is now no far quest of the imagination in art or in life; it has come home to the human spirit. The projection, the spectacle, the remote symbol, have passed; and the new variations, however radical, are therefore not so readily open to outward observation.

# CHAPTER VII

## THE NEW PSYCHICAL ERA

WE hardly appreciate the rapid transformation of human nature, on its highest levels, within a single generation. In this consideration, "the highest levels" are those attained by the great middle class, who constitute the main audience for the best literature—at least, this is the case in America. Thackeray, in his lectures on English Humorists, was addressing such a class in England; and in his lecture on Steele, contrasting the Victorian with the Queen Anne era, he said: "You could no more suffer in a British drawing-room, under the reign of Queen Victoria, a fine gentleman or fine lady of Queen Anne's time, or hear what they heard and said, than you would receive an ancient Briton." The lecturer had just before referred to Tyburn, and remarked that a great city had grown over the old meadows. "Were a man brought to die there now, the windows would be closed and the inhabitants keep their houses in sickening horror. A hundred years ago people crowded to see this last act of a highwayman's life and make jokes on it."

Not more than one-half of the time during which that change had been experienced[1] has elapsed since these statements were made, yet it has sufficed for a change far more remarkable, and which, because it is not outwardly so obvious, is therefore all the more radical.

In the brief period since the sixth decade of the nineteenth century more has been achieved in the material progress of the English race than in its whole previous history, and the most important result of this progress has been such intimate inter-communication as has broken up isolation. There was precipitated—not caused, but permitted—a new era of psychical evolution, involving something far deeper than an increased refinement in manners— a revolution in human thought and feeling, a changed attitude toward life and the world, the creation indeed of a new psychical sensibility, to which must be referred those determinations of the imaginative faculty which have given rise to recent variations in literature and philosophy and to a radical readjustment of all the arts in their relations to life and literature.

[1] The change in refined sensibility which made public executions abhorrent had really taken place within a decade. As late as 1840 Thackeray contributed an article to *Fraser's Magazine* on " Going to See a Man Hanged," in which he described the execution of Courvoisier at Newgate, attended by "forty thousand persons of all ranks and degrees—mechanics, gentlemen, pickpockets, members of both Houses of Parliament, street-walkers," etc. A similar change in public sentiment marked the same decade in New York and New England.

# THE NEW PSYCHICAL ERA

The political historian dates modern history from the rise of the middle classes in the fifteenth century. The psychical historian must date it from some point a little later than the middle of the nineteenth century, when the human reason and imagination, following the course long before taken by science, broke with all forms of scholasticism, of traditional authority, and of merely notional thinking. Metaphysic was henceforth doomed, and all attempts at a logical explanation of life, present or past, were discredited as sterile and unprofitable. Kant, organizing what the Scotch metaphysicians had attempted to describe and logically define, had already determined the limitations of the human understanding and the inevitable self-contradictions of its judgments in any speculation transcending the narrow field of practical human experience. Appearances had been shown to have a validity which did not inhere in any mental inferences from them— as Copernicus had long ago demonstrated—and science had confined itself to the study of phenomena, preparing the way for the evolutionary philosophy, which marked the beginning of modern psychics.

Imagination turned upon its own past creations, which had followed the suggestions of a myth-making or speculative fancy and had partaken of their fallacies. What was true—not logically or mathematically, but vitally true—was alone interesting. The new literature was born with the new knowledge and with the hunger for it of that comparatively large audience which in the course of material progress had been brought under its appetizing and stimulating influences.

Even in isolated communities every child of the middle class in England and America had received some kind of schooling, and for two hundred years the English-speaking people had enjoyed representative government, free from the royal absolutism which in the sixteenth century both the Renaissance and the Reformation upheld as a necessary condition to national organization, but which, when that necessity ceased, had yielded perforce to parliamentary control. In 1850 three-fourths of the people of England and Wales could read and write; and in the Northern and Western States of the American Union there was a school in every hamlet. The exploitation of enfranchised masses for the benefit of the few was impossible. Yet the isolation was sufficient to hold in secure crystallization the general thought and feeling, until steam and electricity broke down every barrier and permitted the free mingling of all psychical currents, not merely to seek a common level, but to find, in intimate contacts, reinforcement, inspiration, and illumination.

Thus recently have we experienced this great renascence, coming without observation, not sudden—it is yet in its mild spring-time—and far from universal, since only those who hunger and thirst for the new knowledge may be filled. The most radical of all revolutions, it has been unattended

by violence. No authority could withstand or pun-
ish what was itself supremely authoritative. The
conflict between the reason of man and his faith
was a thing of the past, even before reason had been
purged of sophistication and faith of its unrealities.
Human imagination and human faith found the same
centre of harmony by the self-same movement. The
whole psychical atmosphere was cleared of abstrac-
tions which had inhabited and dominated it for
centuries—the Powers of the Air.

The new sensibility is a sensibility to reality—
that is its positive characteristic. What is distinctive of it is its psychical apprehension of reality un-
disguised and relieved of sophistication. It calls for
a literature having a corresponding character and
distinction. A superficial realism like that of Defoe
would not meet this demand, and the more refined
realism of Maria Edgeworth, Jane Austen, and
Susan Ferrier is for us only less superficial. The
nearest examples to be drawn from the past are
Mrs. Gaskell's *Cranford* and George Eliot's earliest
sketches and novels, because these are so simply
and sympathetically real. But for these and for the
exceptions already made of Meredith and Hardy,
the break of the new fiction from the old is absolute.

The departure is as strikingly manifest in other
fields of imaginative literature—in history, in the
essay, in interpretative criticism—as in fiction. In
all, the sophistication which lurks in facile gen-

eralization and abstract thinking is alien to the new psychical mood, temperament, or, as we prefer to call it, sensibility. Even Emerson seems to us aerial. Those from whom the immediately preceding generation derived its most potent inspirations —Coleridge, Ruskin, Carlyle, Macaulay, De Quincey, Emerson—while we clearly discern certain permanent, because essentially real, values in their thought, are to us, for the most part, unconvincing. We respond to a new kind of interpretation in Pater, Symonds, Maeterlinck, William James, and in our later historians, whose distinctive value is that they find truth, in its very place and time, in its own color and form, recreating it in their presentment, just as the new fiction is a fresh representation of life, rather than of the novelist's views of life.

We have come back to the world of appearances, recognizing the truth of the deliverances of the senses, whatever falsehood may have formerly been lodged in mental inferences from them or in fanciful associations with them, traditionally perpetuated. Elemental sensations have been freed from the association with them of human action and passion on the barbaric plane or on the extremely opposite plane of superrefined æstheticism. Our *æsthesis* is one that has been restored to us in its native quality, its pristine freshness, and which thus quickly blends with our psychical life, forming the most cherished alliance in our present art and literature. The

which abounded sixty years ago—stories in which the youth and the maiden occupied the reader's interest from the beginning to the end, excluding other characters except those bearing directly upon the love-affair between these two, favoring or opposing, and admitting no feature or incident which did not either directly heighten the romance or roughen its course? The American novel—after the days of Irving and Cooper and before the recognition of Hawthorne—was usually an expansion of this insipid banquet, helped out by equally crude religious or moral flavors. In accounting for the disappearance of this kind of fiction it is easy to say that the writers grew weary of immaturity. But the change in the sensibility of both the writer and the reader implied something deeper than this. There is no aversion and never will be to young romance. Aucassin and Nicolette will please the fancy till our planet is senile. We see them through a distance, which serves the same purpose as the element lacking in these old-time short stories might have served if it had been present—a poetic glamour such as Harriet Prescott Spofford knew how to use in her earliest romances and has not forgotten how to use in her latest, or a quaint simplicity like that which charmed us in Miss Wilkins's first fiction—any element, indeed, which makes romance really romantic through an appeal to the imagination. The development in this direction since Mrs. Spofford and, later, Miss Wilkins began to write is a transformation of this kind of fiction and implies a corresponding change in the sensibility of readers.

In a sense nearly every novel is a love-story, but the best of them we are not likely to regard in that light, because the romance in them is a haunting implication, as it is in life, not the everywhere explicit argument of the drama. The masters of our present-day fiction, by making everything else and every other interest apparently supreme, intensify the implicit romance—Mrs. Humphry Ward in one way and Hewlett in another, while Conrad often dispenses with it altogether—at a considerable sacrifice of popular favor.

The more mature lover has won a preferred interest just because it is possible to associate with the riper period features of psychical value. Marriage is a higher state of development than courtship and, wholly apart from its practical problems, leads out into the world of real life—into its varied spiritual currents and vicissitudes.

Those primary relations which belonged to the oldest, as they do to the latest, social order are, in our new fiction, transfigured, but only reflect the change which they have experienced in our modern life. All our affections have participated in the psychical renascence. We have become unprecedented fathers and mothers, brothers, sisters, and friends, as well as husbands and wives. The primary passions, and especially those mentioned for deprecation in the Litany—envy, hatred, and malice—are negligible factors except in degenerate life and literature, and we wonder how they could ever have had such prominence in old plays and novels. The ancient villains are no more recognized by us as real men and women than the haloed saints. This new sense of life implies a revolutionary change in human sensibility.

From the extreme modern point of view all the literature and art of the past seems to belong to a museum of antiquities, containing precious treasures, many of which appeal to us and are inspiring, as embodiments of a beauty that is everlasting, and some of which we cherish in our affections. For the most part, our wonder and curiosity are compelled; we are touched with reverent passiveness in the presence of somewhat alien majesties who repel our near approach. Our feeling toward them is quite unlike that with which we regard those embodiments of genius which respond to our freshly awakened sensibility, closing in with us at this immediate moment and leading us on imperatively and with absorbing interest to the next.

Even our favorite old authors whom we would fain carry about with us in our pockets rather obstinately refuse domestication. We exclaim, "Dear old Elia!" and, "Dear old Thackeray!" but, however affectionately we approach them, we find that their faces are turned away from us, and even from the readers of their own time. Lamb's regard is mainly toward Elizabethan times and Thackeray's toward the eighteenth century, which he knew so well and so loyally loved—both of them flatly rejecting even comparative modernity. The less ingratiating of the past worthies of literature are sought by us in their remote heights; they are a part of our store of intellectual delights or necessary to our culture. We read them in our youth and, more or less passively, assented to their immortality, and now—we read them when we have the time; present satisfactions are more sufficing.

But the young of to-day who have the time—or should have it, if athletic contests and the training for them are not too exacting—are they reading the old authors beyond what is required of them in the schools? We have a hopeful assurance of the continuity of culture. If it is not to be through the graduates of our universities, then it will be, as in the case of Curtis and Howells, through young men, in every part of the country, whose thirst for the new knowledge will insure also new interpretations of the past, in history, philosophy, and criticism. That which has served its time and passed away, for all its inadequacies, has in its death yielded its final service for our nutrition. All our great learning is from the study of these dissolutions.

Childhood recapitulates past stages of human evolution; its early sensibility demands old myths and fairy tales, and otherwise in its behalf we make large ravages upon what we have shelved, or laid away in our museum of antiquities. This is a natural preparation for the kind of culture which shall recognize what is of eternal excellence in the imaginative creations of the past and, at the time when childish things are put away, shall most intelligently repudiate old and outworn fashions and symbols. We are all, indeed, "children of larger growth," but the larger growth brings with it a rational discrimination, so that even when, by way of holiday amusement, we don an older and more picturesque vesture and play antiques, we clearly understand ourselves and the whimsical nature of our relaxation.

What we seem most of all to have repudiated in our new literature has really become the most essential part of it. The poetry we seem to have spurned has its renascence in imaginative prose. Every new scepticism, every new insistence upon reality, creates fresh zest and hospitality for faith and romance. It is only some old fashions of these that are cast off. So our new life and literature are animated by the spirit which created the impressive spectacle and processional of the past, though the outward fashions and phases of these have vanished.

While a very large proportion of the literature which is being produced, and which in a general way is styled imaginative, belongs to the old rather than to the new, and perpetuates the old fashions, yet it is in many ways responsive to the leading tendency of our time, and is far in advance of all but the very best of the preceding generation.

When we regard any distinctive human period at its prime—the age of Pericles, of Augustus, of Elizabeth, of Anne, of Victoria—we discover psychical lineaments that suggest comparative modernity, but, with closer scrutiny pursuing the comparison, we should see how far each of these periods falls short of the modernity we know—in its criticism, its scepticism, what it called its common-sense, its conception of altruism, its whole attitude toward life and the world.

Within the memory of men who have reached the age of fifty the human spirit has found its true centre of active development and of interpretation—its real modernity, which does not mean the depreciation of the past, but a deeper and truer appreciation, nor any break in the continuity of culture, which is rather led into fresher and more fertile fields of expansion.

# CHAPTER VIII

## THE FIRST REALISM

GEORGE ELIOT somewhere says that the satisfaction of personal grief by frequentation of the graves of those we have lost betrays a lack of imagination. We might at first be inclined to reply that it is not a matter of the imagination, but of the affections; that the more poignant the sorrow, the more it fixes upon particular things which revive familiar associations. The pathetically vivid reminiscence is a resurrection of an embodied presence, where there seemed such absence, so far serving the office of imagination. But sepulture and everything pertaining to it emphasizes absence, setting a seal upon it, leaving no way open to the imagination.

At least this is the case arising from the attitude of our extreme modern sensibility toward the funereal. There was a time when the article of death was read differently; it did not convey the idea of such absolute separation of the soul from earthly associations or even from its earthly tenement. The attentions of surviving friends were supposed to be really serviceable; above all, certain rites concerned with either the careful preservation of the body, as in Egypt, or, as in Hellenic times, its swift cremation. The passing soul was conceived to be a wanderer, as in sleep, only now in a deeper sleep — a wanderer who might linger or possibly return, who indeed could not quite get away but by the pious help of those he had left behind, and was not even then safe from necromancy.

Along with this ancient conception there was some room for the imagination. The character of Hermes, in his oldest guise as *psychopompos*, or leader of these properly absolved wandering souls, was one of the creations of this imagination. Another was the Court of Judgment. The visits of Ishtar and of mortal heroes like Odysseus and Æneas to the dusky subterranean asylum of the Shades, and the seizure of Persephone, furnished weirdly imaginative themes for the old poets. The way was thus laid for Dante.

But in the very earliest times there were no such imaginative creations. Mythology was of later date. If we could go back to the period when man created a language and before that language passed into its secondary meanings, we should confront the first realism, which was one with the first naturalism. Humanity was nearer to Nature, in the sense of being next to it, of being interfused with it, than it has been at any later stage of development. Thought was immediately next the thing, and the word binding them together involved the least possible interference of a notional concept. Imagination was, as nearly as, in man, it is possible for it to be, direct realization—direct and inevitable as any operation in Nature. It was realization on its lowest level, but at the same time the most complete. Sequences thus close, of thought, word, and thing, without reflective interval, had the fatefulness of hypnotic suggestion.

In this immediate embodiment, or realization, the imagination was creative, within its narrow limitations. There was no free intelligence outside of such imaginative realization, which involved only natural selection. Knowledge was possible only in genetic lines, was confined to that which was native or akin.

Of course it is impossible to conceive of man as possessed of articulate speech and at the same time without some measure of conscious ratiocination, far above that in any other species of animal; but progress in this direction was slow, and we may be permitted to regard it in its earliest stage, the twilight of the mind. The consideration of human imagination in this period is interesting, and enables us better to comprehend it at its opposite extreme in the realism of to-day.

In this earliest period the feeling of reality was a near sense of life—so near that, as we have said, it brought all of man's relations to his kind and to the world he knew within the bonds of kinship. We know, in our time, to what degree and extent Nature holds us in her web through elemental instincts, and how much of our life, in its joys and sorrows and labors, depends upon the associations growing out of this natural bondage; but it is not easy for us to understand the ancient sacrament of kinship which was the ground of the worship of ancestors.

In this estate of humanity we could not say that death was apotheosis—that would imply a discrimination between humanity and divinity which did not exist—but it was regarded not as a diminution but an accession of power. It afforded the culminating moment of such tension as was then possible to the imagination. The last sleep was next to a mystery very different from that imagined by us, which dwells afar, beyond an impenetrable barrier. There was no leap for that ancient imagination to take; the mystery resided in a near presence, as near as the friendly darkness of night, which was now reinforced with new helpfulness for the living.

Naturally there was concern as to where the sleeper was laid—the place of contact with so comfortable a mystery, a shrine, therefore, for visitation, with no vain intent. The dead did not pass but by a step; they made a populous divinely human neighborhood. Every living thing which sprang from Earth's treasury of darkness—tree, plant, or flower—was associated with them, as if owing germinance to their potence, far more intimately than the crocuses coming up in the spring were in De Quincey's mind with the thought of his little dead sister.

There was no lack of imagination in this regard for the dead, which had such reality, with no funereal gloss, a backward and downward look, affiliating more with darkness than with light. It had its compensations, and we see from what we know of it that it was love and not fear that made the first gods. But it was a wingless imagination, limited by a rigidly provincial sense of neighborhood, yet with something of the sureness of instinct, as well as of its blindness, in its close procedure.

When we pass beyond this primitive stage we still find the imagination concerning the dead closely following the course of the human evolution. When the tribal isolation is broken up and the romance of human wandering commences, then the dead become wanderers; the builders of cities give the vagrant souls a fixed abode in the underworld, with such discriminations and judgments as are indicated in the penal codes of civilized communities, and a monarchy on earth suggests a King and Queen of Hades. The old idea of immense treasure was still associated with the dusky underworld, whence our term "plutocracy." The Plutonian realm was even more distinguished for its vast population than for its resources. But the strange feature which arrests our attention in the poetic representations, from Homer to Dante, is the weakness and insignificance of this population, which had waned from the divine stature accorded them by the primitive imagination to the mere shadows of their earthly selves, becoming a throng of bloodless, melancholy ghosts.

Herein we see reflected the great change which had taken place in the human imagination itself, after its divorce from primitive naturalism. Its integrity had been broken. The despotically real earth-thought had given place to a complex and wavering world - thought, prismatically brilliant but unreal. The symbol interrupted the close sequence of the thought and the thing, and the living word which had been the bond of the sequence passed into its secondary meaning or shadowy concept. What wonder that death should be supposed to work the same change that had come over the spirit of life — the transformation of realities into phantoms? In either case, the change was not sudden, but the effect of slow development through centuries.

With the loosening of the naturalistic bond—so tenacious at all times and in all circumstances—man entered upon his proper psychical destiny, with the free imaginative vision and faculty which made art, philosophy, literature, and the higher life possible, but he reached these heights only after long bondage to a symbolism only a step removed from the immediate despotism of natural instincts, and to a rigid social conventionalism. The romantic awakening, the disintegration and emancipation, is first historically apparent in migratory peoples, lovers of the sea, like the Phœnician, who gave the world letters, and the Ionic Greek, who gave it art. The world sense of the Heroic Age, not at all reflective, but æsthetic, and thrilling with free and joyous life, furnishes a natural explanation of the prevailing fancy as to the desolate estate of those in whom the pulse of this life had been stilled. Thus Homer expresses it, when he makes the shade of Achilles say to Odysseus that he would rather be a slave in the upper light and air than King of the Underworld.

Evidently, in the Hellenic view at least, the present world had blurred the old backward regard. Men had come to have reliance upon their own lluminated intelligence, independently of ancestral reinforcement by way of darkness.

The significant note of the primitive realism was the sense of a kinship potent in life and still more potent in death. We see a survival of this in the Hebrew race before the Dispersion, a people shrinking inland from the dreaded sea, repudiating the myth, the symbol, the idol, the image of anything, and whose language was cut down to its roots. For a man to die was to be "gathered to his fathers." Paradise was Abraham's bosom. In the story of Joseph and his brethren we have the simplest and strongest embodiment of the sentiment of kinship.

What we have called the provincial imagination, because of its confinement to an immediately near realization, within limits fixed by elemental instinct and passion, in the Hellenic type of development escaped these narrow bonds, projecting mythological impersonation and legend and, later, the objective embodiment of æsthetic sensibility in poetry and in all forms of representative art. But in all this detachment from Nature we note the lingering domination of the older motives, loosened from the ancient tyranny and softly touched with beauty. In mythology, the earth mother, Demeter, held her legendary place, and her sacred mysteries were still inviolate. The sombre presences of the underworld—the Eumenides, Pluto, Persephone, Hermes, and the rest—continued to exercise their majestic functions. The prominence given to the Promethean myth by Æschylus and, by all the Greek dramatists in tragedy, to human destiny as working in the dark lines of natural relationships, shows, in the brightest era of Greek art, the survival of feelings nearly allied to the primitive naturalism. Nevertheless, the cult of Athene, who of all divine personages was most completely dissociated from the occult influences of Nature, gained ground, and was the inspiration of new humanities.

How inveterate those occult influences were down to the thirteenth century of the Christian era is indicated by the strong hold which, in that second twilight of the mind, the black art of magic gained upon the human imagination, reviving necromantic enchantments and maintaining the ancient conception of an inferno, in which, however, another dynasty had supplanted the Plutonian. The prevalent belief in astrology rested upon the implication that man's life was but a part of the web of a universal destiny, and was determined by the stars under which he happened to be born. The divergence—a noticeable one—from the old naturalism was in the substitution of celestial influences, associated with luminaries, for those which were terrestrial and which worked in the darkness. Nearly allied to this belief in magic and much more closely allied to the provincialism of the primitive imagination was the mediæval faith in reliquary miracles, with this notable distinction: that their effectiveness was due to sainthood. At the very earliest stage of Christian belief, heaven, never before accessible to men, save by special translation, as in the cases of Moses and Elijah, was "opened to all believers." This remote separation of the saints from those everlastingly doomed, or temporarily subjected to purgatorial flames, is in marked contrast to the earlier location of paradise, into which Dives, in torment, could look and have speech with Lazarus. Still earlier there was not this separation; all went to one place. To the primitive imagination the idea of the neighborhood of departed kindred seems to have precluded that of any distinct abode of the dead.

In mediæval pilgrimages to shrines and holy places, in the crusades for the recovery of the Holy Sepulchre, and in knightly quests for the Holy Grail, there was an enthusiasm not only in itself romantic, but one that, as in ancient visits to the Delphic Oracle, helped to develop a cosmopolitan or world sense which would finally dissipate the essentially provincial regard for any shrine or oracle. The mediæval world sense of politics, as distinguished from the modern national sense, in its very cosmopolitanism, and in the favoring atmosphere which it created for the development of art and the humanities, helped to make the Renaissance inevitable and effective.

The first realism was, on its purely naturalistic plane and within its insulated channels, intensely vital, as sure and relentlessly direct as instinct, as Nature herself. The imagination shaping its course had the values of its integrity—its defects were in its limitations, precluding the possibilities of art and of the higher humanity. Our departures from this primeval integrity have made human history—the record of human strength and weakness. Fallibility, not, as in instinctive procedure, mere limitation of faculty and vision, but positive vacillation and failure, has attended every step as the indispensable condition of advance. The objective realization of beauty in art stands out more firmly than anything else in the retrospect; but the realization of truth, in politics, literature, philosophy, and dogma, brings into view a long procession of masquerading phantoms—some of them fixed in ghastly permanence, while others appear and vanish, showing as much worth in their falling as in their emergence. One set of symbols is forever displaced by another, and there is a distinct value in the expedition of succession.

To loiter with the old symbol, to cherish the lifeless token, like lingering at the grave of one who is not there but has arisen, is to put mere actualities in the place of realities. The actuality was one with the reality in the primitive naturalism; to us it is, or should be, a trivial accident. To cherish the pen which belonged to a great writer or with which an important document was signed, the sword of an eminent warrior, or the ship which he led to a decisive victory, the room in which a poet was born or happened to die, or any other relic, betrays a lack of the historic sense as well as of imagination.

The symbol which has played so important a part in thought and art is something more than a relic or token, something to be justly interpreted in its set time and place and for its relative value. Words themselves are symbols, directly in their origin, and with indirect and notional meanings in their secondary use; and it is in these notional meanings that we must beware of their phantasmal tyranny. So any symbol may have its despotic misleading as well as its helpful leading. It is the ready tool at once of true wisdom and of false sophistry. Modern science has by a jealous caution in its own field led the way to a new realism in which the imagination after long bewilderment has found its true centre of harmony

with the natural and human world, a world which—
if we may follow to the end the line of thought with
which we set out—no longer harbors ghosts or ghost-
ly trivialities.

It is the world sense, uplifted and illuminated,
which has triumphed over the unreal phantoms of
the mind and over the Powers of the Air and of
Darkness, embodying thus a free Christendom following the spirit of the Master. The near sense of
life is realized in a brotherhood not confined within
the bonds of natural kinship, as we hear the Master
ask: "Who are my brethren?"

Rousseau and Nietzsche were bewildering prophets, falling far short of this new realism. What
shall be said of those critics who would call our writers
of fiction from their world of psychical realities back
to a masterful handling of elemental passions? Natural relationships have inspired some of our finest
fiction, treating of home and homely things. These
relationships have themselves been psychically uplifted and refined above the elemental plane. Our
new humanities are developed in that superstructure.

# CHAPTER IX

## THE WORLD SENSE

OUR culture is, in good part, the appreciation of the new realism, in which life is concerned even more than art, philosophy, and literature. The world sense of the imagination, as distinguished from its old earth-bound or provincial sense, has not only created this realism, but has liberalized culture. Often, it is true, realism is spoken of as if it were confined to the near view of life and things, as if, indeed, it were simply the result of close observation and of a feeling for local color. It does very distinctly involve a near sense of life, the feeling of neighborhood which makes it intimacy, the genuinely altrurian miracle of knowing a thing by becoming it; but we lose sight of its chief distinction if we ignore the light of its seeing and the charm of its feeling due to the sense and knowledge of far away things—the cosmopolitanism which makes it always widely and wisely human.

That ancient collocation in the Prayer - book phrase, of "the world, the flesh, and the devil," no longer holds. We have a different world now, which has conquered the other members of that partner-ship, or at least put them on their good behavior. If not completely renovated, it is so far transformed in its main currents that we would share its fortunes, renouncing only its pomps and vanities, as required by our baptismal vows. There was, indeed, much to renounce—much of vanity, pretence, and false-hood; but the world itself has done a good deal of the renunciation for us, not only helping us in the divestiture, but making it difficult for us to revive the old worldly fashions without seeming unworthy or ridiculous, and our present concern is lest we be not worldly enough, after the new fashion, with which the best of us find it hard to keep pace; and this concern has developed a new conscience in us.

Special organizations do not help us to apprehend or express the world spirit of to-day. They may have legitimate objects not otherwise attainable; but every arbitrary system has its vice, its per-version and limitation of truth, its peculiar shib-boleth. There is more of comprehendingly sym-pathetic socialism outside of socialistic organizations than there is in them. In England and America a political sentiment which is not rigidly partisan determines the critical issues of politics, having a quality which lifts it above the abuses incidental to party organization. The growth of humanism, while it owes much to institutions which have had spon-taneous origin and development and has its expression largely through these, is quite independent of all special organizations deliberately planned and conducted and distinctively labelled. The world spirit has moved where it listed, marshalling all human elements—even the passions of men, in the mass, and individual ambition—for its own ultimate issues. The old fashions it has outworn were its garb for their season of service.

Custom has always in its origin expressed as much of the truth of life as human sensibility could at the time apprehend, and thus became the ground of institutions. Isolation tended to preserve in crystalline stability all the outward forms and fashions which at once registered the measure of intelligence and arrested its growth. War, which to-day the world sense justly denounces, was the vehicle of change and progressive movement, and moreover, in its natural course, while beginning in repulsion, ultimately widened the scope of attractions and of the higher amenities. It was the precursor of commerce. The harvests of peace were sown in blood; and the shedding of blood in contention was followed by the blending of the blood of the contestants for broader kinship. The growth of the humanities was an illogical drift, through organized associations that were reconciled antagonisms, harmonies from the resolution of discords.

The *pax Romana*—the consummation of centuries of warfare—was not allowed to corrupt the world;

there were outlying barbarians to harass, to provoke fresh conflicts—enough of them in Europe alone to finally conquer the stablest of empires and to be in turn conquered by its old law and its new faith, whence another blend of races and, after a period of fierce and intimate fusion, another leap in the growth of the humanities—that is, in the growth of the world sense. The wonderful achievements of the thirteenth century in the fine arts and the technical; in education—through the establishment of great universities—in political organization, as manifest in the Italian cities and in the rise of the British Parliament and the signing of Magna Charta; and in literature, as exemplified in the poetry of Dante and in the shaping of the great national epics, the Cid, the Arthur Legends, and the Nibelungenlied, show what were the possibilities of the human spirit even in the Middle Ages and at a time when the greater part of Europe was in the clutch of the Tatar. Dr. James J. Walsh has made a striking array of these achievements in his recent book, *The Thirteenth, Greatest of Centuries*.

But really the most remarkable distinction of that century was the contest between Pope and Emperor for the temporal sovereignty of the Christian world. The significant fact, irrespective of the merits of the conflict, is that the culmination had been reached of that order of world politics in which the people had no voice or responsibility. All conflicts, for any merit there might be in them or in

their issues, awaited a more profound development
of the world sense in its peaceful evolution.

The substitution of national for world politics in
the sixteenth and seventeenth centuries, though it
restricted and intensified patriotism, was not a reversion to isolated provincialism. Like the growing
tendency to individualism, it indicated a deeper
and more pervasive world sense; but there were
difficulties which this sense had to meet and overcome—such as class privilege and prejudice and the
narrowness of sectarianism in religion.

It is only within a generation that we have had
that clarified world sense of which Matthew Arnold
was a true apostle, and against which no Philistinism
can prevail. Arnold perhaps laid too much stress
upon the healing virtues of conformity; whereas in
the toleration of dissent is the surer path to better
agreement. It is the progress of science which has
really led the way to a culture the full meaning and
value of which is in seeing things as they really are,
or at least above all things to desire such vision.
Science, in its largest sense, the knowledge of real
procedure in natural and human phenomena, has
not only given a firm basis to our contemporary
realism in historical interpretation, creative criticism,
and imaginative literature, but has suggestively determined its method. It has extended the limits of
human thought beyond its mundane scope, so that
the world sense has widened into a cosmic sense, in-

cluding the feeling of the unity of all life and the recognition of universal kinship, thus making provincialism forever impossible by the destruction of its "hole and corner" refuges and of the notions and fancies bred in these. This enlargement of the imagination, giving it the freedom of the universe, is its full emancipation.

But, in the field of art and literature, the world sense of realism, the true feeling of Nature and humanity, is sufficient without availing of those wonderful disclosures which are strictly scientific, and which by themselves more than compensate in psychical value and interest for the fabulous wonders they have displaced. The scientific specialist has often himself narrowed and minified the truth in his own department of investigation by a kind of provincialism incident to specialization, or by an atrophy of vision, making him blind to a living Nature and to the miracle of a continuous creation, and thus shutting him into a mechanical universe. Imagination, in literature, owing much to the clarified atmosphere of the world prepared for it by modern science, yet takes its own open way, always in contact with the main currents of human life.

It is especially fortunate—but only recently so—in its freedom from alliances with special causes and therefore from polemics of every sort. As, in our new and redeemed world, war is no longer an organ of movement, but, outside of partially civilized races, an anachronism, so from imaginative literature all contentions are excluded, relegated to their peaceful resolution in the natural course of things. This kind of literature takes no label. It is not specially socialistic, democratic, didactic, or even realistic. Thus it entirely escapes provincialism.

The world sense is a very different thing from what is called common-sense, which, in its genesis and in its obstinate survivals of old notions and habits, is essentially provincial. We are not considering the reactionary eddies, or even the floodtides, of Philistinism, but the main current of human thought and feeling which has already become dominant, to which every critical change in history has been tributary, and of which all changes to come will be the reassuring triumphs.

The old order of life and literature passed more than a century ago, and now its vestiges have disappeared — all its masks, heroic, dramatic, and rhetorical; behind which lurked old stock notions, with impressive suggestions of majesty, appealing to their counterparts in the minds of those who witnessed the spectacle. Of course these phantoms are still on parade, but they do not appeal to the general intelligence.

The world sense implies the true historic sense which distinguishes between ideas and facts, between reality and the perfunctory actuality which survives it, and which the old aristocracy sought to perpetuate

—the meaningless token of past majesty, surviving from idle habit that aristocracy itself. But this world *geist* which has created for our time a new sensibility, and thus the new realism, looks forward rather than backward.

Our real literature has therefore no stock-in-trade accumulated from old stores. It has even dismissed old locutions. This renovation of speech is in itself an interesting feature to the reader who is observant enough to detect subtle changes in phraseology— the displacement of overworked introductory and conjunctive clauses and the departure from traditional syntactic forms. These are mere details, but they show the surface drifts of thought, apparent in the craftsmanship of an artist like Mr. Howells.

Writers of this order may have mannerisms, but these are at least individual; they have for the reader who is familiar with them the consistency which is noted and expected in the expression of a friend's face and in his gestures, original and free from pose. The manner, distinctively real and true in the novelist himself, loses these qualities when, as in some of the most striking of R. D. Blackmore's fiction, it becomes the manner of speech of the characters in the novel. The authorship of a paragraph written by Henry James, speaking for himself, would be detected at once, but the conversations in his stories are detached from his individuality, thus sustaining the reality of the characterization. The dramatic poem, or drama in poetic form, has always been at a disadvantage in this respect, compelling the absolute detachment of the writer from his work. Henry James keeps the personalities he creates quite within the reach of his constant and pervasive individual interpretation.

In the writer's scheme, before the new realism was possible, his detachment, like that of a showman, was necessary, since the spectacle must go on in its own very much predetermined way—predetermined, that is, by the limitations of the audience for which the entertainment was provided. The traditional legends, fancies, and prejudices already stored in the minds of that audience, along with elemental passions, fixed within narrow channels the author's theme and procedure, from Homer to Addison. The sense of actuality, concentrated upon certain fixed facts, memorially cherished, and upon events, personalities, and circumstances of time and place associated with them, was keenly developed. Some authors of transcendent genius, accepting the limitations and the precise leverage upon the human mind afforded them, made palaces of these prisons, as some artists bound to fixed symbols yet realized the everlastingly beautiful. Those who, like Plato, rose to the realm of ideas, addressed the few and, in their discourse, were still entangled in the meshes of inveterate fancies which they could not wholly escape.

Not before our own time has there been an absolutely clear and transparent medium of communication between the writer and an audience which for extent may be called general, and which may be said to have general intelligence. It is the imaginative author's supreme advantage to have no preconceived vantage-ground to stand upon and, on the part of his readers, no prepossessions in his way. No accommodation is expected of him. His path lies clear of possible collisions and of occasions for allusive coquetry with vanished illusions. He need waste no time or energy in mental athletics or in clever conceits, need have no epigram in waiting or even a conciliating anecdote. The sensibility of a large audience, developed by the world sense, awaits his disclosure of truth as he sees and feels it. This audience is upon his own level; it is not necessary for him to write down to it, and any didacticism on his part would be an impertinence, as any showman's trick would be an insolence. What part could the old-fashioned plotting of a story have in meeting the high curiosity of such an audience? What has high-pitched rhetoric, overwrought passion or pathos, any forced exaltation or depression, to do with its proper satisfaction?

All this is by way of negation — of reference to elements excluded from the advanced imaginative literature of to-day. If our readers want a positive example of the extreme advance in fiction, they will find it in Henry James's stories. Other examples, not involving the same keen vivisection of our modern life, would serve for illustration, but Henry James's fiction is ultimate in its exposition of the possibilities of a high psychical entertainment—so different from that furnished in the literature of the last generation that it belongs to a newly discovered continent of genius. His style is not as many who are baffled by its complexity and involution suppose, an affectation either carelessly or wilfully assumed, but precisely adapted to his method and purpose; and this spontaneous adaptation has developed with the culture of his art. He lets nothing pertinent to a given psychical moment slip away from his flash-light illumination of that moment. That is the extreme opposite of the narrative style, where incident follows incident *in tandem*, and separate sentences convey circumstances that belong to a single view. This disjunction does not mar the story whose interest depends upon incident, but in the delineation of a pregnant psychical situation it dissipates an effect which depends upon perfect co-ordination. If the study of such a writer is severe, it is but the complement of what has first been the writer's difficulty, and may be undertaken by thoughtful readers as part of a liberal education. It is the more worth while because the situations presented, however complex, are plainly and appealingly human. The difficulty which the reader has to overcome arises out of the real situation and finds solution there — very different therefore from such difficulties as George Meredith often arbitrarily puts in the reader's way, through conceits referable only to the author's mental caprice.

The complexities in the imaginative field of the new realism are those which belong to the reality itself of our life in its extreme modernity, and they lead to the plainest simplicities of our literature—such simplicities as have been brought into our practical economies by complex scientific adaptations of physical forces, giving us the electric light, telephone, automobile, and motor-car. Through what seemed like an irrecoverably broken integrity of life, the life of the world has been assembled into a new harmony and has found its psychical integrity. If we could realize for ourselves what was formerly styled the simple life, if we could return to Nature and be again immeshed in her web, we should have no comprehension of humanity or of Nature.

# CHAPTER X

## THE HIDDEN PATTERN

A GOOD deal of affection is mingled with our gratitude to writers who love the past and who have the creative power to restore it for us by giving its living reality fit embodiment and at the same time true imaginative interpretation. Lamb and Thackeray are more lovable to us because, though not caring for us, they looked back with so fond a regard to the life and literature of preceding centuries. It is this that we cherish most in their mood and humor, and, lacking it, their writings would lose their most endearing charm and lasting value. We do not so much care for the information they convey. With them that was merely incidental. Lamb's sensibility was thrilled by the fresh and buoyant pulse of life in the Elizabethan time, with a response to its imaginative creations so accordant and sympathetic that his interpretations seem like the divinations of a familiar spirit. Thackeray, more consciously an artist, and more detached, was to a like degree sympathetic with the eighteenth century, giving us not a chart but a picture of it, penetrating its intimacies so deeply that he truly reflected its elegancies, and beneath its beruffled and bewigged exterior disclosed its sincerities, to which with all his heart he responded, yet leaving a fair and fresh field for the new appreciations of Austin Dobson, who has thereby inherited his due share of the affection we feel for his predecessor.

Ours is a very self-sufficient era, looking forward rather than backward, but finding abundant occupation, inspiration, and satisfaction within its own fertile and amply developed domain, in no way dependent upon tradition for the course of thought or the conduct of life. The knowledge of Greek is no longer indispensable to the Baccalaureate degree in our colleges, nor technical scholarship in matters of antiquity to a liberal culture. Yet this age, which in every main current of its life has broken with the past, is, more than any former age has been, in love with præterite humanity, as the newly made bride yearns for the home from which her face is resolutely averted.

Not exactly like that, save for the resolute aversion and the yearning. It is not a sentiment which makes old things—old faces, old scenes, or old songs —dear just because they are old and familiar. It is not a religion, like the worship of ancestors. There is in it no link of direct association as between youth and maturity in an individual life, making vibrant the note of reminiscence which Du Maurier so often struck in his fiction. Nor is it an idle play, as with the strange toggery of an old attic. It is a strong passion like that which archæology has become to us moderns—not for facts, but for meanings.

To the imagination nothing human is alien—and behind us lies an indefinably long stretch of humanity. We may find only portions and parcels of a dreadful past, but we resent unfamiliarity and seek reconcilement. We look coldly upon any man to whom an outworn fashion has therefore become insignificant, and we doubt his new faith if it has awakened violent hostility to old faiths. Truth which has made us free has also given us a comprehension of old masteries and old slaveries. This trait, which is distinctive of modern imaginative interpretation, has been characteristic of nearly all the masterly creations in literature—of all that, by virtue of their general kinship with humanity, still compel our reading. Cervantes, the worthy contemporary and almost peer of Shakespeare, is the elect of our hearts from all Spanish writers because, in the first great novel ever written, he showed his love of the chivalry he parodied, intensifying its essential idealism while playing havoc with its mock heroic fashions.

We have proved our sympathy—the passionate ardor of it—with an older humanity by such interpretations as Pater and Symonds have given of ancient and mediæval life and of the Renaissance, and by the warm regard in which we hold these writers, along with Andrew Lang, who so easily turns from illuminative appreciations of Hellenism to some new disclosures of the virtues of the Pretenders or of Mary Queen of Scots, and to the praises of the author of *Waverley*.

Ever since the new modern criticism began—from Sainte-Beuve to George Woodberry — the sympathetically appreciative attitude toward an older time has been maintained without any sacrifice of our modernity, or rather as one of the noblest manifestations of the modern spirit. Our histories have been rewritten, accordant to this dominant note; too often, before our time, they were written in advocacy of some special plea, political or religious. It is surprising as well as significant, how many and remarkable revisions have been made within a generation, correcting monstrous and persistent traditional misrepresentations.

No writer bound by class prejudice can truly present even the excellences justifying his own cause; much less can he truly portray the defects of a cause in conflict with his own. It was impossible for us, therefore, before we had broken with tradition, to really comprehend truths which tradition disguised rather than supported.

We are only repeating what Thomas Hill Green expressed years ago in a profoundly philosophical essay on the "Value and Influence of Works of Fiction," when we say that the novel has been one of the principal agencies through which class prejudice has been gradually undermined.

Other forms of imaginative literature—poetry and the drama — flourished under the old aristocratic order, in relation to which they were subsidiary dependents and, in their high tension, participants of its pomp and lofty stateliness. The novel has fulfilled its sympathetic mission unconsciously and therefore more effectively; but it has done this only in so far as it has been a real representation of life. Much that it has consciously attempted, with set plan, has been unreal, and unfortunately its wide appeal to a lower order of intelligence has been based upon this unreality. For this reason our fiction has not experienced the same thorough purgation as our historical and critical interpretation of human life. But the general tendency of the fiction of our day, on whatever level it may reach the popular mind, is toward reality. The general intelligence is ever more and more responsive to the catholic and sympathetic note of that advanced criticism which, while it accepts all of humanity in its real significance—the past as well as the present, leaning with mingled awe and tenderness to old sovereignties and old loyalties—yet resolutely repudiates all formal judgments and set canons for the regulation of life and art, and all prejudices and fixed notions which rest upon tradition or upon our own loose thinking.

Life does not yield itself to our study. Accurate observation and close attention to detail do not characterize the attitude or suggest the temper of mind with which the novelist meets the human phenomena of his own or of any other time. Study contracts the spirit, dulls sensibility, and leads often to loose thinking and shallow feeling. Love, passionate curiosity, a sympathetically tentacular sensibility—to these all worlds, spiritual or material, past, present, and to come, yield the romance of discovery. The novelist communicates his discoveries in the very terms in which they have come to his own vision. He obeys the injunction which George Eliot put upon herself, and which she expressed in reply to the suggestion that she should write a novel based upon sociological data—"not to let the picture lapse into a diagram."

The diagrammatic habit came in with logic, and has no pertinence outside of the narrow scope of human adjustments subject to arbitrary volition and design. The lines thus rigidly drawn are not those of life in man or nature; a single pulse of the living world shatters the whole plan. When Portia comes into court, Shylock's demand for exact justice suffers derision. When the Lord utters His parable of the Judgment, we ask what has become of the decalogue? In no logical scheme of the universe could it be in the natural course of things that the innocent should suffer for the guilty—but so it is in the real world.

Yet from the beginning man has sought to superimpose his diagrams upon life and the living world

—to his own confusion. He is saved from his own logical absurdities only by the fact that his own life is one with that of the universe, woven according to a pattern hidden from his conscious observation. So far apart are rationality and reasonableness.

It is just those notions which we hold as certitudes, whether as obvious to common-sense or as infallibly established by studious logic, that are convicted of falsity and shallowness in any real vision. Even Euclid's axioms are contradicted in the higher regions of mathematics. The man with a paradox has his prosperity and welcome because of our underlying conviction that only by the inversion of obvious maxims are living truths disclosed.

The creative imagination, though in every age the servant of human misconceptions and prejudices— as Apollo tended the flocks of Admetos—has softened the hard lines and covered confusion with beauty; readily inclining to the hidden pattern of life's making which, in final reconcilement, proved to be that also of its own weaving.

Now is the day of that reconcilement. Our present culture means above all things submission without reserve to the mastery of life—of life as it is and not as we loosely think it ought to be, or as we would in the dry air of reason have arbitrarily devised and fashioned it.

It is not in the schools, by the acquisition of special information, that the imaginative writer is equipped for his ministry of communication, but in sympathetic contact with the pulsing, vibrant life of humanity. Never in any former age was such a culture possible to him: in nature, in literature, in the inspiration to be derived from the main currents of the world about him.

So much has been restored to him that was formerly blurred or eclipsed—faith, romance, the beauty and glory of the world—that what seemed disillusionment becomes, to his clearer vision, revelation.

As we have seen, the past he has broken with is nearer to his sympathetic comprehension than it was to the men who lived in it. He can now, as men never could before, accept Nature not for didactical suggestions or sophistical analogies, or reflections of human sentiment, but for what she really is in herself as a living organism; for what science has disclosed of her rhythmic harmonies, yet divesting these of formal predicaments and evolutionary phraseology; and for her never failing charm, in the infinite variety of plant and animate life, in the unpremeditated motions of cloud, wind, and stream, and in the varied gradations of color and tone. Best of all, she belongs to the kingdom of grace, with no response to merit, but quick for healing and merciful ministries.

This is the same Nature which from the beginning has wooed the human soul, not less invitingly because inarticulately and in many ways persuasively, but now for the first time frankly accepted. The wooing by Artemis of Endymion is realized, divested of the mythical disguise. The flowing lines of the hidden pattern shown in Nature are seen to be complementary to those that same pattern—so unlike our diagrams—has been shaping in our human life; the gracious descents of the material world—whose own ascensions are invisible to us—correspond to the risings of humanity.

In like manner is this human life restored to and accepted by us on its own living terms—in its happy and inevitable altruisms which displace those of busybodies and meddlers, — in its uplifting, which is better than our hard and brittle rectitude,—and in its generous spirit which judges not nor abstractly separates between the good and evil so inextricably mingled in the temperament of both the human and the natural world. Is it not in this way that the Master's gospel also has been restored to us for our real apprehension?

The distinctive value, for the writer, of this modern culture is one derived immediately from life in humanity and Nature, and not from any formulation of truths about life as the result of study or studious observation. Our culture depends upon the growth of faculty and the evolution of sensibility, resulting in real knowing and real thinking, as well as in true feeling. The glosses which have been put upon our own life and that of Nature are removed, and the significance of the partnership of man with the physical world from the beginning is disclosed.

Because the general intelligence has been to so great an extent illuminated by this new culture, the imaginative writer has the supreme advantage of a large, ever-widening appreciation and response to a real representation and interpretation of life. There is no restriction upon his field, so that he hold to the living truth in theme and method, following living lines, and eschewing the loose thinking engendered by formal study—such study as often enters into what is falsely called idealism, thus "sicklied o'er with the pale cast of thought."

It is not necessary, and certainly it is not desirable, that any writer in this or in a coming generation should choose to do just the thing which Henry James does—least of all any other kind of thing in just his manner. It is enough if he can see as plainly and have the same passionate desire for truth. There will always be writers—at least until we have reached the millennium of culture which, to the most optimistic expectation, is yet very far away—who will prefer effectivism to reality, appealing to the crude tastes and unwholesome appetites of the less thoughtful reader, or who will flatter stiff-notioned Philistinism. We have in Maeterlinck the example of a mind growing in the processes of its creative work from the fitful and uncertain fancies of his early dramas to the highest levels of speculative interpretation. But usually the line of distinction separates writers according to aims, false or true, dominating their work from first to last. Maeterlinck, even in his faltering first steps, saw the radiance of a living truth which illuminated his instabilities, and which has grown into the clear, full light of his later day.

No living theme is excluded from fiction by modern realism. The reality is in the writer's vision rather than in the selection of this or that particular theme. He must see plainly, without colored glasses or magnifying lenses, or — to get away from the physical metaphor—without notional distortion.

This kind of realism surrenders many striking effects possible to the showman's artifice, and many that are natural in the untempered expression of primal passions. Undue emphasis and exaggeration, cumulative magniloquence, and the falsely pitched note of enthusiasm in literature have fallen into contempt, even on the stage, as they have in oratory and in all forms of expression. We resent declamation and reserve the "Marseillaise" for revolutions. We are mastered by the note of our plain, common life, and our art is subdued to a natural compass of exaltation, as in the most highly developed music. This is not a "development of plane surfaces." The harmony is chromatic, complexly broken, and therefore has unlimited variation of expression, yet preserving a natural dignity. Reserve has always been essential to art; it is our Hellenic heritage of culture; but this term does not adequately characterize our modern mood in the best prose any more than it does in the best music. The chromatism, affecting the content, whereas reserve affects the form, of expression, is distinctly modern. In music we might call it a division of tone, in painting a division of color, in response to the more complex culture of hearing and vision. In a general way we might call it a more divided living and thinking, in response to the more complex culture of sensibility. Or we might use an evolutionary term and call it advanced specialization. But this is all a kind of diagrammatic explanation of something eluding explication—something which we apprehend in its own living terms, and which we see growing into these terms in the modern course of life, literature, and art.

Every personage, divine or human, in Homer's poems comes before us with a single epithet, which is repeated with each reappearance of the character. In later literature there is an equally inflexible typical delineation. Coming down to a period nearer our own, let us compare a novel by Fielding with one by Mrs. Humphry Ward. The vast difference is not more apparent in superficial portraiture than it is in the meanings of life, hidden from the earlier and abundantly disclosed by the later novelist. Life itself has changed in the interval separating these two writers—changed in what it is to human thought and feeling—more than Nature has to the human comprehension of her mysteries through the revelations of science; and the development of imaginative sensibility has been both a part and a product of the transformation. Mrs. Ward is probably not a greater genius than Fielding, any more than the intellect of Herbert Spencer was greater than that of Aristotle, or the creative power of Tennyson mightier than that of Æschylus. What has happened to the modern world—just this world of ours to-day—is new life, along with a new sense of it, because of truer vision and real thinking.

• Something creative in this, not the result of study or close attention to detail, has wrought the transformation, lifting life and sensibility to a new psychical plane, and disclosing an infinite variety of hitherto unsuspected phenomena—a play of activities undreamed of before. To reach this chromatic harmony it was only necessary to accept life on its own living terms, instead of imposing upon it terms derived from our notions, conceits, fancies, prejudices, or any kind of sentimental predilections, and arriving at what we call "views" of life as distinguished from the real sense of it.

It is this real sense which, on the psycnical plane, has introduced to us a new continent whose altitudes and depressions are not determined by primal seismic violences, but come within the gamut of sane thought and feeling,—yet by no means therefore a level world; and the charm and infinite variety of the phenomena thus disclosed, and furnishing the rich content of our new literature, more than compensate for the towering eminences and yawning abysses of the continents left behind us. We do not regret our atrophy to old shocks and obsessions. Our new histories do not disappoint us because they sacrifice impressively dramatic and spectacular effects to real disclosures, nor our new fiction because it depends for its interest less upon striking plots of construction and pronounced traits in characterization than upon a really significant representation of human life.

The best fiction of to-day has really more of constructive art than that which preceded it, though this art, following the lines of life rather than an arranged scheme, is not manifest in obvious features. It has more varied traits, instead of a few emphatically pronounced or merely typical features. It has a deeper dramatic interest, intellectually and emotionally, though the drama itself is so changed to follow the pattern which life itself makes, yet in its course unfolding novel surprises. Above all, it has more spontaneous play of human activities and a finer and more vital humor—not the specific humor which excites to laughter or even suppressed merriment, but which, like every other quality of the modern art of expression, is pervasive, without losing articulate distinction, concurrent with the ever-varying course of the writer's thought and feeling. Humor, in this sense, is the most distinctive quality of life—the index of its flexibility, of its tenderness, mercy, and forgiveness.

# THE HIDDEN PATTERN

As we accept Nature for what she is in herself—so purely for this that we prefer to consider separately the results of scientific investigation concerning her processes—so we accept life on its own terms, disregarding philosophies of history or any formal scientific theories concerning human phenomena.

This attitude saves the imaginative writer from taking himself seriously or—what is the same thing—presenting life in rigidly absolute terms which reality inevitably contradicts. There are no straight lines in his procedure, and what notionally is called a plane becomes in his geometry spherical, as it must in a real world. Seriousness is too much a bewrayment of life to be confounded with sincerity. In its dulness and lack of vibrancy, it is as alien to sorrow as it is to joy—to the tragedies of life as to its comedies. The great masters in literature have eschewed it, whatever their other defections from the truth of life. John the Baptist was "serious" when he thought to set the world right by the rectification of human accounts, the payment of dues, and reparation for injuries. He came fasting, but when the Master came, eating and drinking, the friend of publicans and sinners, this formal scheme was dissolved in the good Lord's humor, showing the hidden pattern.

# CHAPTER XI

## THE MODERN URBANITY

SIMPLICITY is more an urban than a rustic quality in our modern humanity. It is indeed the noblest achievement of civilization, associated with all that we esteem the finest fruits of human culture—freedom and breadth of thought, catholicity of sympathy, truth of art and life.

This was not perhaps quite so evident a few generations ago, when it was the fashion to assume that the city must be perennially redeemed from effeminacy and corruption by the accession of fresh blood from the country. We should now unhesitatingly say that the salvation of the country has all along been the accession of urban influences. A cycle must be in good measure completed before it is clearly understood. Many of our fixed maxims pertaining to policies and economics are derived from ancient history, and have to be reversed for any application to our own time. Even in the ancient and mediæval world it is clearly enough seen that the history of the city is that of civilization. The oldest cities are ruined or stagnant, and we know the story of the causes of their decadence, but each bequeathed some precious legacy to the world.

The modern city belongs to another order. It does not exist for the glory of an individual sovereign or of a class, or for the exploitation of all outlying humanity. It has not within itself the seeds of inevitable decadence. It rises in fresh vigor with every new generation. The country looks to the city and to the university, which is a concentration of a city's highest values, for its inspiration and uplifting.

We no longer hear of the artificialities of urban life, which during the last half century seems to have undergone the same transformation as our imaginative literature—the same divestiture of sophistication and unreality. The banalities and frivolities of the vain and empty-headed survive, alike in town and country, only with more opportunity for their senseless display in the urban environment, perhaps to a greater extent than they do in the giddier sort of literature, which is more sensitive to the contempt of the thoughtful; but, for thoroughly plain men and women, without pretence or disguise, who exemplify the true modern idea of the simple life, we look to the urban rather than to the provincial type.

The period of this transformation which has given us a new urbanity has been precisely that which has brought to its consummation the vast organization of commerce and industry, and the mastery, for human uses, of the forces of Nature. The parallelism is significant. This florescence of material progress would give us only food for pessimism if there had not also emerged, in corresponding impressiveness, the mastery of the human spirit in quick reaction to the materialism, which was thus confessed to be a part of the evolution of that spirit. All we ask of this last phase of that complex social and material organization which it is the office of the modern city to create and promote is that it be catholic, sane, and, in the largest sense, humanly helpful; and the general resolution to make it and keep it that is essentially a part of this whole high and supremely modern transaction. The main and most significant consideration is that the immense leverage upon circumstance gained by this progress means facility and opportunity—the release of the spirit for the noblest uses and purposes of life.

The merely outward spectacle of our metropolis to-day may seem massively imposing, and one whirled along by the elevated railway on the lower east side of the city catches glimpses of architectural effects which rival in picturesqueness the cañons of the Colorado; but closer acquaintance discloses delicate and ingenious devices for ease, economy, and expedition, which appeal to a finer fancy, suggesting the spritely offices of a new and unmythical Ariel, who is as deft in social as in business service. Who can estimate what up-town apartment residence has done to simplify the life of young married couples?

Yet it is not so very long ago that the finest spirits in literature, like Ruskin and Carlyle, were berating this modern progress, and had a large and sympathetic following. It was not that they thought to find the simple life by going into the woods. They were lovers of the city, and it was the disturbance of urban life—the violence done to its old and picturesque aspects—which they chiefly deprecated. All great writers, and especially the poets, have been haunted by the beauties of old cities. Tennyson missed the humors of London streets, and would have more frequented those streets if he had not been so easily recognized that every flower-girl would beg "Mr. Tinnison to buy just one little nosegay."

The amenities of life are of urban genesis and culture. As Lady Montagu truly said, "People mistake very much in placing peace in woods and shades, for I believe solitude puts people out of humor and makes them disposed to quarrel."

A great city is itself no small part of the culture of a young writer or artist; it is at once the fountain and the haven of the Humanities in art and literature, rich also in monuments and historic associations. Human life at full tide offers itself in limitless variety to the sympathetic mind and heart; and sympathy itself is the deepest note of urban sensibility. Every great city has, moreover, its individual mood and temperament, gathering to itself the children of its own feeling and genius.

All this praise is due to cities of the old order, under the aristocratic *régime*, which, despite the vices and artificialities due to an unwholesome refinement—such as denatured Paris at the middle of the eighteenth century and evoked from Rousseau the most sophistical of tirades against sophistication —still appealed to the poet and humanist. Has the purgation wrought by the more healthy modern sensibility, and completed, as it could not otherwise have been, through comparatively recent triumphs of science and material organization, made our cities less alluring?

Certainly in some cities it has had this effect upon the æsthetic sensibility. Charles Lamb, "revisiting the glimpses of the moon," would be able to find more of his old London, with less violent derangement of the familiar perspective, than Henry James recently could discover of his old New York after twenty years' absence. Yet this distinguished novelist, for all his keen disappointment from the disturbance of personal reminiscence, could not be psychically insensible to many a novel humor and agreeable surprise.

It must be confessed that, in the modern movement, the cities of most rapid recent growth have lost much of their old urbanity. But they have developed suburbanity, and have made urban the vast outlying territory. Hence the automobile— one of the most obvious tokens of the simple life, in our modern conception of it—is a familiar sight on all country roads; and the manifest improvement of public highways has been largely due to new means of locomotion, beginning with the bicycle.

In the times just preceding our own, eminent writers and artists seem to have clustered in groups. Indeed, this is a very old habit in the centres of culture, in cities and university towns; we can point out these stellar groups in the galactic drift of the centuries from Athens to Edinburgh. From the early years of the eighteenth century certain distinctively recognizable groups of writers established and sustained by their contributions periodicals for the popular diffusion of culture. The mention of Addison, Dr. Johnson, Professor Wilson, Sydney Smith, Robert Southey, William Hazlitt, Leigh Hunt, Tom Hood, and, in a later generation, of Dickens, Thackeray, Leslie Stephen, and Froude, brings to our minds at once not only distinct aggregations of authors bound together by intimate association, but the reviews, monthly magazines, and literary weeklies which were the reflection of their thought and their time.

There are no such closely blended associations of writers in the England of to-day, either for concentration of literary influence through periodical publications, or, independently of any special work of this kind, such a group as the Cambridge "apostles," consisting of friendly thinkers like Tennyson, Arthur Hallam, Trench, Spedding, Maurice, and Sterling. Nor in American centres are there any successors to those old affiliations existing among authors in New York in Bryant's, Irving's, and Whitman's time, or in Boston and Cambridge in the days of the old Anthology Club, out of which came the *North American Review*, or later when the most notable of all American literary constellations shone first and for a few in the pages of the *Dial*, and afterward for the whole country in those of the *Atlantic Monthly*. It is within our memory that the Lyceum lecture system was a kind of national institution, but it was supported by a score of eminent writers who, whether they came from Philadelphia, New York, or Boston, would have needed no personal introduction if they had met by chance in Ticknor & Fields' "Old Corner Book-store."

Now, in England and America, the club has taken the place of those old spontaneous affinities. This remarkable change in the social habits of writers has come in the natural course of evolution through the urbanization of the whole country. The writer to-day knows no local centre and courts no literary affinities; he does not even care to be considered a literary person. His affiliation is with his readers. The absence of any professional guise helps to simplify his life as a free and plain personality, and in his relation to other human beings whom he desires to know simply as plain men and women. He is at home everywhere, without any disquieting apprehension of being recognized as "the great This or That," content to have broken with greatness of any kind, with every labelled distinction.

The social habits of the whole people have suffered a corresponding change. Progressive urbanity promotes readier and wider sympathy, not dependent upon domestic or local relationships, or even upon previous acquaintance. The family is not held so closely together in the old way, and the urbane relaxation of an often irrational lien has refined the relationship, giving it more beauty and friendliness, with reasonable concessions to individuality. Narrow circles, cliques bound together by common tastes or prejudices, have been broken up. Interests larger and more varied have become common in a more general sense, delocalizing community itself. One is not embarrassingly concerned because he has not been introduced to another; if prompted to comradeship, he easily yields to it on the simplest terms, as readily as he would dive into the pages of a new author. Young people who never met, all over the country, are corresponding with one another with graceful familiarity. This could not have happened, naturally and as a matter of course, a generation ago.

Literature in all its forms, from the novel to the newspaper, has, more than anything else, widened the sense of community. Fiction has made every genuine character we meet interesting and companionable. There is little reading of it aloud, which was a common family occupation fifty years ago. Each reader's occupation is with the writer, and with a host of writers. He no longer needs the Lyceum lecture, and does not especially care to see his favorite authors on the platform; the personal curiosity is narrow in comparison with that higher curiosity which impels him as simply a reader, and which is so abundantly and variously satisfied.

To this general urbane sensibility travel is no longer necessary for either its stimulation or satisfaction—would indeed limit experience to the observation of mere actualities, and destroy many a beautiful illusion created by writers out of elements which escape the notice of the casual tourist. The desire for travel is stimulated by these writers and our journeys through the world made more pleasurable, through the association of actual scenes with the far more significant pictures they have made for us, but our imagination, thus revivified, still depends, for all the most important values, upon a previous impression, involving much that is absent from actual vision.

Does the American writer miss something which foreign writers seem to have ready at their hand from the deeper cleavage between classes and the consequently more marked distinction of outward traits? Some of Thomas Hardy's most characteristic work is in his masterly portraiture of the peasant—the best in English fiction, better than Scott's of the corresponding class in his own country, excellent as

that is. But we have no such class in America.
Yet our story-writers have made the most possible
of rustic local color and character, of pioneer life,
of every provincial trait; more eagerly perhaps because of the paucity of material.

We have never had any really close and downright native provincialism in the United States.
The types that seem to us most provincial did not
inherit that character, but have acquired it through
prolonged sequestration in comparatively inaccessible districts. Our earliest settlers sought the new
continent, some of them impelled by the spirit of
adventure, but most of them by the desire for freedom. They were people with formed characters,
obstinate convictions, and strenuous determinations
—not a plastic race from which one would expect a
renascence in art or literature.

These limitations, intensified by the exigencies of
a straitened environment, narrowed American lives
through several generations, but in the channels of
expression rather than in those of sensibility. While
creative genius was manifest in statesmanship, we
can see why the production of masterpieces in
literature was so long delayed. Not thus narrowly
determined was the American sensibility to literature or to influences from the main currents of the
world's life. Early periodical literature in this
country existed mainly to meet the eager demand
of readers for selections from the best current English
essays and poetry, and to satisfy their keen curiosity

concerning European events. Especially toward France the general attention was turned at the opening of the revolutionary drama, and even in Boston, where Federalism was dominant, the sentiment of *égalité* was so fanatically adopted that to many the modest title of "Mr." seemed repugnant and gave place to "Citizen," and it was a subject of discussion in the newspapers what less awkward word might serve the same democratic office as "Citizeness" in place of "Mrs." When Bryant was the one American singer to respond to Wordsworth's note, Byron, Shelley, and Keats and the Lake poets were as joyously acclaimed by American readers as they were derisively criticised in *Blackwood* and in the *Edinburgh Review*. In the next generation Macaulay's essays in the *Edinburgh Review* were collected and published in book form, as were De Quincey's, in a score of volumes, and Thackeray's *Yellow-plush Papers* and Carlyle's *Sartor Resartus* — which was still-born in *Fraser's*, so far as English appreciation was concerned—years before these authors were thus honored in their own land. This quick and keen sensibility was developed not merely in cities and towns, but in country districts and in new Western settlements and mining camps.

The Westward movement carried with it the progress of the nineteenth century, was an expansion of Eastern culture. Even the sharp traits of pioneer life rapidly disappeared. The sensibility was not merely national, it was cosmopolitan. What used to be called, in a peculiar sense, our Americanism is no longer a sought-for distinction, and we do not now look for "the great American novel."

This urbanization of the country does not tend to uniformity. The old outward idiom — the settled form of dialect, tone, and manner—whether in city or country life, was the result of a crystallization which is now impossible. The modern simple life, accentuated by its complexity, is forever flowing into infinitely varied manners and humors—traits of the spirit—thus offering to the writer of fiction a richly diversified humanity, with adventures and excitements of a new order. Since it is a so wholly urbane field, it does not matter whether the writer finds his people in the city or in the country. If Holman Day takes us into the woods in *King Spruce*, it is the human flavor and not that of the woods which we relish. The theme need not be urban so that it is really and plainly human, though it is only to the urban sensibility of readers that such rustic sketches as Muriel Campbell Dyar gives us could appeal.

# CHAPTER XII

## THE INEXPLICABLE IDEALISM

THE aspiring young writer, however patiently he may have followed us in our study of imaginative literature, will not be able to derive therefrom any helpful guidance to worthy achievement in that field. More than ever before it is a chartless field. The old sign-posts are of little avail to point the way to an author in the courses taken by the new literature. They still stand, and writers mindful of them follow well-worn paths, attaining canonical excellences and, often, notable successes; but the appeal of these writers is to readers whose taste and sensibility are confined to traditional grooves.

The extremely modern literature and the advanced sensibility in which it finds response repudiate the old maxims. Conscious aspiration, with deliberate aims and methods, is not nourished in this atmosphere. Doubtless the heart of youth forever echoes the sentiment expressed in Longfellow's "Excelsior" and in the Virgilian "Sic itur ad astra," not from any desire to reach the highest altitude or, still less,

any astral goal, but because life in its tension is uplifting—a rapture, with indefinite sense of the whith-
erward. But the ascension is not open to observation, and only in its descent is there an expression
of life. "The banner with the strange device" is
not in distinct evidence. Isolated grandeur offers
no temptation to the modern writer, whose mind
is set not on getting up in the world, but in getting down to it in frank and neighborly intimacy.

This disposition does not make for that kind of
thing which is ineptly called the democracy of literature, but for a new and genuine aristocracy, in
which mock sovereignties are displaced by the real.
This is indeed the outcome of all civilization—the
emergence of a natural and therefore tolerable aristocracy. What was formerly styled aristocracy was
but a vain show, dependent upon no lasting basis,
but upon the temporary and insecure leverage afforded by unnatural social and political conditions,
which, because they were inevitable, gave it its sole
justification—that of necessity; and of this the most
was made, if not the best. Of the whole fabric of
ancient and mediæval aristocracy all that remains
is what was created by the imagination in art and
literature, ennobled by what was best and sincerest
in life, yet warped in many ways through association with the false notions of a distorted humanity.
Such real sovereignty as there was in this old order
was vested in human genius, creating in life that

culture of the mind and heart which was to develop a new humanity, and at the same time creating those works of the imagination which, surviving the evanescent phenomena of this development, remain to us as its lasting memorials.

This everlasting aristocracy it is which, after so many renascences, has emerged, freed from its old bonds and impediments, for the leavening and uplifting of our modern life through the sovereignty of human genius, to whose meanings and powers all our progress and institutional development are subsidiary. Why should we call it a democracy? A free and intelligent people repudiates demotic passions and instincts, which really had more force in that old false aristocracy which compelled and at the same time was obliged to conciliate them; in a free society there is neither opportunity nor plea for their exercise. This real people—fortunately a majority of the whole mass—is not merely submissive to law and order, but, through a more or less deeply developed psychical sensibility, has desires and interests belonging to a life which transcends ordinary social, political, and economic functions, and which indeed is a cultivated garden enclosed within the protecting walls of inviolate conventions. In this garden of human culture it is the life of the spirit which abounds, as truly, in all its shapes, the creation of genius as are the products of the imagination in art and literature. Civilization exists for it, and it is all of civilization that survives.

In this, the essential, life of a people, the term "equality" has no meaning; perfect freedom makes it insignificant. All value is associated with some real sovereignty. Life has growth, increase, therefore authority. Living excellence and charm are compelling, and of all things this compulsion is most diligently courted. Whoever can impart psychical inspiration through new disclosure of truth, in vital embodiment or interpretation, and not as mere information, is eagerly recognized as master. Discipleship is the passion of cultivated minds. We are proud of what has been accomplished for general education, but the culture of the general sensibility is a more important factor in our modern civilization and determines the value of education itself. One may be educated to the extreme point of efficiency in every department of knowledge and not have this culture—not have real knowledge, real thinking or real feeling, or that higher curiosity which creates the zest for new discovery, new romance, new faith and hope. On the other hand, one may have this culture with very little of what is commonly called education beyond the ability to read. The time was when the chief motive for teaching children their letters was to enable them to read the English Bible; what was not unwisely considered the most important channel of culture was thus laid open. In our day this simple ability to read will bring any mind, whose higher curiosity is awakened, into all the main currents of human thought and feeling, and may give it satisfactions not experienced by the most erudite, whose studies do not promote the creations of genius or their comprehension.

If we go back, and it is not so very far back, to the time when peoples were illiterate, we find no such spontaneously determined popular sensibility, none that we could properly call psychical. The communications of genius were quite entirely confined to impressions conveyed by art. The sovereignty of genius was itself limited by its alliance with other and arbitrary sovereignties, and it was popularly accepted along with these as part of the imposing and majestic pomp of that old order of humanity. Then came the drama—at first as a kind of literature for the illiterate—exaggerating every feature of the masquerade, and finally, when there was an audience for it, literature itself, which now has come to be the readiest and most significant means for the popular expression of genius. Discipleship has now a new meaning—that of minds moved from their own centres, rejecting imposition, seeking the masters of a new magic whereby the plain things of life are invested with their native nobility.

The older arts sought detachment from life, a distinct place apart, and a duration boldly contrasting with life's brevity. Imaginative literature in its new forms, like music, in its later development, comes nearer to life—a spontaneous communication, as frank, intimate, and pervasive as the sunlight.

It assumes no fixed memorial shape and has no alliance with traditions to help it on to another generation. This is one of those characteristics of modern realism which seem to justify the academic Philistine's oft-repeated allusions to the mediocrity of our current literature.

Genius in literature has come to be just what it is in that portion of our life which may be called "the good part," since it is not "troubled about many things" that present themselves as problems in the manifold relations of human existence. Imaginative literature has a closer intimacy with our essential life through its renunciation of the argumentative and of any distinctively teaching or preaching function, confining itself to the embodiment and interpretation of life. As in the climbing of genius there is no conscious aspiration toward the "life sublime," so in its genial precipitation its expression is simple bounty rather than conscious ministration.

Human existence forces upon our observation numberless needs and miseries appealing to our sympathies, but the ministration to these in perfect good-will falls far short of any positive expression of life in that world where the Humanities transcend humanitarianism. It is a limitation of love to meet only need, use, and the obligation of pity. Even martyrdom seemed to St. Paul a limitation. On the other hand, vital altruism, the sense of universal kinship, is the ground of all creative communication and expands to the full compass of its meaning.

Nothing is more distinctive of modern life and literature than its sympathetic quality, which has its pure and natural manifestation as elicited by the pathos inevitable to a mortal and fallible race rather than by singular instances of suffering, cruelty, or crime. But the sympathy most characteristic of the bounty of genius is that of comprehension, whether the conditions involved be happy or painful. Happiness, ease, comfortableness—these are not the qualities of life which have imaginative values, nor do such values inhere in the want, wretchedness, and deformity which excite commiseration. The concern of genius is with the life of the spirit in its reaction upon the world—upon every sort of conditions—whereby it comes into its own psychical kingdom of grace, play, and humor, mingled as these must be in a texture which is above all things simply human, with the joys and pains which have run like bright and purple threads through every web woven by the imagination from the beginning. But, as expressing the bounty of genius, there must be the grace, the play, and the humor. Take these out of life and literature, and the whole field falls into sterility—there is no garden.

Grace, we say, rather than beauty, for the latter term is often misleading in its suggestions, indicating some outward perfection rather than a spiritual quality. Too often this outward perfection has no more spiritual significance in our conception of character than it would have in our regard of physical features, as when we think a life beautiful because of its faultless symmetry from a formally moral point of view—a symmetry which completely masks the personality. Humanity is so inevitably fallible that any formal perfection seems unhuman. The faltering note appeals.

The avoidance of formal perfection is a distinctive mark of modernity in literature. It is because of a revolt from regularity of measure that prose is developed in our time rather than poetry. The tendency is more evident in the form and structure of literature than in its themes. Always poetry and romance have depended upon human fallibility for their poignant interest. It is true that in a good deal of recent fiction the departure from beautiful conditions has passed to the opposite extreme, to the portrayal of ugliness, and, while malignant motives have been banished, excessive stress has been laid upon the faultful side of human nature. But we are more impressed by the general tendency of writers, so deep seated that it seems an instinct, to abjure forms of excellence which only a generation ago were held to be canonically imperative.

One important feature of this change in fiction is the abandonment of elaboration in plot and in style. The structure of a story has lost the prominence formerly given it, is hidden as far as possible from observation. The reader does not expect, indeed he resents any appearance of, a contrived arrange-

ment of circumstances to produce a dramatic effect;
he experiences not only disillusion, but a kind of
humiliation, as if he had been played upon. He
would rather forego the satisfaction of even agreeable surprises and happy conclusions than that
these should be mechanically brought about, and he
certainly will not forgive the writer any arbitrary
infliction of torture, whatever ingeniously devised
relief may be held in waiting. The complete and
perfect arrangement, once absolutely demanded in
the story as in the play, now suggests unreality.
It is the insistence upon reality which has effected
the transformation in fiction and which in literature
generally has led to the rejection of the old-fashioned
rhetorical elegances of expression. Spontaneity and
reality are inseparable.

It is just here that play and humor, as main
characteristics of modern genius, have disclosed their
imaginative values in the new realism. What we
have called "the good part" of life, its essential
field, is independent of all studies, problems, or dis-
puted questions. Here humanity is one with nature, having no offices, but an infinite variety of
manifestations that cannot be defined in terms applicable to those efforts and economies which we
usually style the serious business of life. Genius
here, in its embodiments and interpretations, oc-
cupies no transcendental field lifted above common
life; it is that life, indeed, with which it is wholly

concerned—with all of it, in its real meanings and natural procedure, for its true representation, not for its explication, and for the disclosure of its ever freshly emergent variations in the evolution of spiritual physiognomy, thought, and feeling: all in the familiar earthly setting and shot through with the pains and delights naturally incident to human earthly existence. The play is not for levity, nor the humor for risibility—both are implications of a real and spontaneous human nature.

The new fiction is, therefore, so intimately engaged with life in its natural manifestations, lifted by culture to a psychical plane, that its old devices are not only no longer necessary, but are impertinent and meaningless. The lack of formal completeness in structural elaboration is an excellence rather than a defect; and this passing of the planned scheme has given the really significant short story a new precedence. The novel must justify its larger compass, not by its intricacies and complications, but by its larger psychical scope. The old fashion of extending a story to the dimension of a novel, through a more or less arbitrary elaboration of the plot or multiplication of characters and situations, is no longer tolerated by cultivated readers.

What especially forces itself upon our consideration is the fact that genius is creative not merely in art and literature, but, first of all and most of all, in life—not in the life of the few, but of the many; not in the life of chivalry, of the soldier, of any conspicuously great hero, but in plain human lives. To be plainly human means a great deal in the way of culture. It is impossible to the unthinking and even more impossible to the sophisticated. It is the condition only of those whose minds have been swept clear of old idols by the main currents of modern thought, and that yield no tribute to the mock-heroic and the mock-sublime. Thus there has come to be a large body of plain people who are simply human and whose lives are real. It is in these real lives alone that genius finds the fertile ground for its garden of the Humanities. Here grace, play, and humor abound. Genius in literature is not the reflection of this bounty, but its express manifestation.

We apprehend the reality of life in the play of it rather than in what we call its serious business. Longfellow's "Psalm of Life," striking the serious note, fell far short of the true conception. A contemporary of the poet, Horace Bushnell, then, next to Emerson, the most original of American thinkers, in his Phi Beta Kappa oration at Harvard, sixty years ago, rose to a higher note, when he said that all work was for an end while play was an end in itself—that play was the highest exercise and chief end of man.

There was reality of life in the old order—the play and humor of it, therefore; more always in the life of the ignorant Barbarian than in that of the sophisticated Philistine. But in our day the reality has an unmasked, undistorted expression, in a clear and not in a prismatically colored atmosphere. Sophistication seems to be a middle world, perhaps we may call it purgatorial, through which humanity must pass before it can attain spiritual freedom—that is, the free play of spontaneous being, action, and feeling. Reality in this freedom is the ground of a true idealism. Here the good is not relative—good *for* something — nor absolute, since it is not an abstract quality, but simple goodness and, like the beautiful and true, inexplicable, with all reason in it but no reason for it.

We are baffled when we seek explanations of certain aspects of modern life which seem to our common-sense whimsical and absurd. Why do hard-working parents send their daughters to the piano instead of the kitchen and sacrifice themselves to give their sons respite from drudgery? It is not mere fondness, nor is it simply ambition. A psychical temptation which did not appeal to older generations allures to life worth living for itself—to the inexplicable idealism.

Some ineffable, undefinable charm invites us all. Native to life, whatever the conditions, it has found in our modern life the conditions for its full mastery and bounteous expression. It has mastered our literature, giving it a new investiture, another art, too natural to seem great.

# CHAPTER XIII

## THE NEW ART OF PROSE

WE speak in a general way of the art of prose literature without being able to say just what it is, and the better the literature the more difficult it is to define the art of it. The *ars poetica* is instantly intelligible, at least in its outward forms. The imaginative values which we demand of the poet belong also to prose; but in the modern novel or essay of the highest imaginative order we find nothing that exactly corresponds to those formal obligations which the poet, the sculptor, or the painter cannot escape. In what sense, then, is modern imaginative prose an art?

Surely, we think, there must be an art of fiction, and we are reassured of this by several able treatises in which the development of this art has been traced from the earliest story writing to the novel of our own time. But, whatever light these careful analyses may throw upon the course and progress of fiction, they do not help us in those extremely modern instances of writers who have discarded all the canons that were formerly considered indispensable

272

to the art. Even as to past examples, what is presented in such works is not their art, but their place in the course of a merely technical development.

If we say that it is imaginative values which constitute the art of any work, we may be on the right track if we are able to discern just what kind of imaginative values distinguishes the prose of to-day not only from that of any other period, but from all creative work in earlier times which we have been accustomed to call art. For it has been the fashion to think of art as something separate from life. In the plastic arts, in painting, and in instrumental music, the artist worked *in alia materia*, in marble, color, and tone; but this difference implied no contempt of life any more than man's other uses of Nature did—it was but the mastery of materials for the expression of his creative imagination, a reinforcement of human possibilities, an expansion of the scope of art beyond the limit of bodily expression in dance and song and in dramatic representation.

So far art would seem to have been an enhancement of life, an outward translation of its tension. It is when we regard the theme that we see how life was belittled in the presence of the old art, dwarfed by alien grandeurs, eclipsed by an unnatural radiance, overmastered by a remote tension. The earliest choric and lyric forms had in their violent ecstasy been linked with the terrible spells of superstition. In later creations of his imagination man was forever projecting a monstrous superman which outfaced and overshadowed him. In the more subdued embodiments of Hellenic art and in those of the later art which was of Hellenic inspiration, while there was a freer play of human genius and more perfect expression of the beautiful, associated, at least in sculpture, with the human form, still in the theme the superhuman guise was dominant; gods and demigods strode alongside man and, in stature and deed, overtopped him.

In the Iliad mortals are but the tools of the gods. Homer presents a few plainly human groups, and from his description of Achilles' shield we may infer that in relief work of that kind representations of the familiar scenes of every-day life were not uncommon. It is true, too, that the gods as portrayed by Homer are themselves swayed by human passions and subject to human frailties, but this is mere mock-humanity. In the whole range of ancient and mediæval art, including what is classed as the greatest poetry, from Homer to Milton, the projections of the imagination are not in simply human terms and do not disclose simply human values.

The unhuman and superhuman disguises, reflecting distempers of thought, fancy, and feeling, make the old arts and poetry seem alien to us. We may deliberately build a new cathedral, but, after all, it is an anachronism. We cannot revive the spirit that inevitably expressed itself in the erection of these edifices, which to mediæval peoples were their homes more intimately in thought and feeling than

were the houses in which they dwelt. The masterpieces of mediæval painting appealed to souls pre-
occupied by a strange other-worldliness, and portrayed humanity under stresses only monstrously
imaginable. These are far away from us, who are
seeking to know what our world really means for us
in all its possibilities and what are the real values
of human existence. A painting like Michelangelo's
"Last Judgment" is as impossible now as a poem
like "Paradise Lost."

It is not strange that we should turn aversely
from the old art—not from its beauty and formal
excellence, which have an everlasting appeal to
æsthetic sensibility, but from its meanings, which
seem to us so remote from reality. We are haunted
by its beauty, the embodiments of which we cherish
—repeating eclectically old forms of architecture in
our own, gathering together in galleries the originals
or copies of old statues, friezes, and paintings—to
awaken or keep alive the sense of the beautiful in
every new generation. The study of these embodiments, however divorced they may have been from
all that seems to us really significant in human life,
is an important part of our study of the Humanities.
The evolution of the creative imagination is indeed
paramount above all else in human history in its
appeal to our intellectual interest; apart from what
it is as a disclosure of genius, it registers civilization.

Confining ourselves to the extremely modern period which is identical with the new psychical era,

we find that there is a new art as well as a new literature. The plastic arts reached their highest perfection centuries ago, and we only repeat old forms
in fresh combinations. But painting has had its
modern transformation along the same lines as literature, abandoning traditional disguises and symbols. The impressionistic tendency prevailed at the
same time in painting as in poetry, fiction, and other
forms of imaginative prose; and both in art and literature the tendency persisted in so far as it yielded
true imaginative values. The art of painting has
been applied to the interpretation of the past during
the last two generations with as much fidelity and
devotion to the truth as the best novelists have
shown in that field. Abbey is as painstaking as
Hewlett, and his genius is as spontaneous. Land-
scape-painting is giving Nature her true investiture
—that which is purely her own—not merely following pre-Raphaelite suggestion. The work is creative, discerning in things their soul and temperament, unveiling the charms that Nature woos us by.
Painting has forsworn allegory; and religious sub-
jects are no longer treated symbolically.

The drama considered as an art—that is, something for stage representation—has won its recent
distinctions in the lines of the new realism.

It may perhaps be fairly claimed that in painting,
the drama, and poetry certain features distinctive
to modern prose were first foreshadowed—that the
transformation in these arts, involving the divesti-

ture of old fashions and the prophetic intimations of a psychical renascence, was going on long before it was apparent in fiction. This is undoubtedly true in the case of poetry. The relation of Wordsworth to all that we recognize as modernity was more direct and intimate than that of any novelist in his generation. Browning was the chief inspirer of the great prose writers of the last fifty years. The influence of these poets is felt more in prose than in poetry. That is the significant fact, showing that the tendencies they intimated naturally found a freer and ampler expression in prose than in their own field of art. If poetry, because of its form, has a recognized limitation, the representative arts are still more restricted.

More than any other art, music, in its modern development, aligns itself with the imaginative prose literature of the present era. Of course there can be no direct comparison between these so different kinds of expression; but we think of music along with literature because of the pervasive intimacy of both in our modern life and culture. It seems as if music were forever striving to become articulate, and as if literature, in its furthest reaches, sought to express meanings beyond the range of any vocabulary. While music is under an obligation more precise than that of any other art—one that is exactly mathematical—yet, because it inhabits not space but time, it seems to escape definite confinement. It can be communicated by printed signs, carrying in these its exact architecture, and be as widely re-produced as any form of publication, suffering no such modification of values as is incident to the re-production of painting. It has varying degrees of exaltation, but it has this advantage over literature and every other form of artistic expression, that it can never be degrading. Its development, which has been alongside that of modern prose, has shown a like variety and amplitude of expression, and in each the appeal is more and more of a psychical character, in a region of sensibility where meaning and feeling are inseparably blended, without notional alloy. The transformation in the art of music from its earliest to its present appeal has been concurrent with that of human sensibility itself. From its old obsession of the feet it has become a modest and even tentative seizure of us, taking us as thought takes us, lingeringly, hesitantly, waiting upon our souls. Is it not in this way that our best prose novel and essay appeal to us?

The art of pictorial illustration in black and white, while it has achieved notable triumphs, especially in periodical literature, in the graphic representation of our every-day life, and in sketches of travel, has done its best for fiction, in the portraiture of char-acter, giving extreme visualization to the imagina-tive creations of the novelist. The artists who have succeeded Cruikshank, Tenniel, Doyle, Du Maurier, and Leech, and whose work is so familiar to the readers of our foremost illustrated magazines, have done their part toward a plainly human portraiture of life, and they have not been merely the followers of writers in this advance. They might, perhaps, justly claim that they led the way—that they were the first to abjure insipid types of merely physical beauty, the first to depend confidently upon unliterary intentions and values; and this confident dependence is the chief distinction of the best contemporary fiction.

While a general, or at least casual, survey of the art of the past brings vividly before us features and associations which are alien to us, and thus likely to beget aversion, especially when we reflect upon the remoteness of this old art from the plain realities of human life, yet our closer regard shows a modern transformation—which is, after all, only a marvellous sequel of less striking changes that were going on from the beginning of civilization—a transformation like that which has been effected in human life itself; and we see that we have changed, and art with us—that we have a new art because we have a new humanity. The earlier projections of the imagination reflected life, but with refraction, as in a mirage, because life itself had not found its centre and therefore had not attained its true realization; thus it must have had its tension and exaltation outside of itself, taking, in all forms of art, shapes that were magnificent and imposing but unreal. Now that life has come home, art is homely.

So, after this brief survey of those kinds of creative work which it has been the universal custom to call the fine arts, and the consideration of that radical transformation whereby these arts have responded to our modern psychical sensibility, thus becoming an intimate part of our present culture, we come back to our original question: In what sense is the imaginative prose of to-day an art?

If we were considering the fiction, the histories, and the interpretative essay before the middle of the nineteenth century, we should find very little to even suggest such an inquiry, and the little we might find—say, in Addison and Steele, in Lamb, Hazlitt, and De Quincey—would be so different from our new literature, so allied to an older order by formal elegances or rhetorical devices of style, as to be hardly pertinent to our immediate purpose. It would not occur to any critic to speak of the art of the Waverley Novels. Down to the Victorian era, and in the case of very much of the fiction of that era, the novelist was limited—even Jane Austen was—by the superficiality, or, we might better say, the externality of the theme; the treatment was of human life, but confined to obvious features, traits, and situations. There is the same style of treatment in a good deal of contemporary fiction, a theatrical exaggeration of external features often serving for effectiveness and rather cheap entertainment. It may be called art, but it is a poor species of that old art which depended for its effect upon false similitudes.

When we speak of the art of Thomas Hardy, of

Conrad, of Hichens, of Mrs. Humphry Ward, we mean something quite different—something so unlike the older art that we must say that either it is not art at all or a wholly unprecedented art.

The very content of the art, the kind of human phenomena emerging at the stage of psychical evolution which we have reached, is unprecedented. All the old signs fail us; the well-worn tokens have given place to an ever-fresh coinage. The creations of the human spirit are wholly its own, born of it, not made in conformity with any logical proposition or mental notion, and they bear no stamp of extraneous authority; whatever of divinity they may have is in their purely human genesis. The whole meaning of that designation—"the son of man"—is restored to a humanity which nearly two thousand years after the advent of the Gospel has come to the worldly instead of the other-worldly or saintly acceptance of it. "The fruits of the spirit" are not limited, as to their nature or their scope, by the narrow definition imposed by puritanical or any other arbitrary judgment as to what is the chief end of man.

If we were going on in the old way, making much of myth and of traditional fancies and symbols and customs, seeking dramatic effects that are only outwardly impressive, courting empty but picturesque splendors, our imaginative literature would still continue to create the art which has always been associated with a distorted similitude of life. But this is not the gait of that humanity which, almost within the limit of two generations, has emerged, taking its own shape and growing into its full stature on the psychical plane, with interests and desires that find satisfaction only in humanly real issues and values.

In the vast field thus opened for a new employment of the imagination in the embodiment and interpretation of a real world and a real humanity, our prose literature most intimately and pervasively appeals to the newly awakened sensibility. It deals with phenomena so different from those which engaged the genius of earlier times that old canons have gone meaningless as the old fashions have become obsolete. The writer stands so near to life that his imagination takes the tension native to that life, along with its real feeling, shape, color, and rhythm. This is the new art of prose.

But apart from this general designation of the art there is also to be considered that which gives it its infinite diversity through the individual genius of the writers. The new conditions, unlike the old, break up conformity and compel individuality of expression. Our writers are not grouped in classes or schools. Whatever characteristics they have in common belong to the new attitude of literature toward life and the world; but each one sees with his own vision and according to his native powers, his comprehending heart and feeling mind. Here we touch upon undefinable possibilities.

Prose has this advantage over other arts, that

while these can exist only as each meets its formal obligation, it alone can dispense with the rigid forms of outward tension without disintegration. In this relaxation lurks also its peril; disintegration lies in wait for it, through the loss of vital tension—of the inward pulse, tone, vibrancy, which belong to life. Another danger is in the treachery of its medium of expression—the ease with which a word or a phrase, under the misguidance of a too ready fancy, may blur or displace reality — the facile generalization which blots out the values of the particular.

The novelist, while avoiding refraction in his representation of life, must give objectively the reflection, however subjective his impression, and, though shunning the stress of the theatrical and the picturesque, must present the dramatic movement and picture, learning from the old masters clear and firm delineation, lest his work seem less real than theirs.

# CHAPTER XIV

## PROSPECT OF IMAGINATIVE LITERATURE

THE distinction made by De Quincey between the literature of power and that of knowledge—that is, of information—though often quoted by writers of to-day, was more pertinent to his own generation than to ours. He began his literary career when in poetry a new creative era was at its height, while in prose the didactic habit of the preceding century still persisted, especially in the writings of philosophers and men of science, whose speculations and discoveries were conveyed in strictly formal terms as much in contrast with the quaint and imaginative discursions of Bacon and Sir Thomas Browne, three centuries earlier, as with the illuminative expositions of Clerk-Maxwell, Faraday, Tyndall, and Herbert Spencer a generation later. With the writers of our own time in the same field, such as John Fiske and William James, the contrast is still more striking.

It would never occur to us to call a formal treatise literature in any sense. Yet analysis, description, scientific exposition, criticism, and narrative, which, as formally presented, do not belong to literature, may by imaginative power and insight be lifted to that dignity, while the novel, which ought always to have that exaltation, may be an utterly feeble and insignificant production, or, even if interesting and important in its matter, being devoid of imagination, may fall short of the distinction.

There is really no literature but the literature of power, which in our day covers an immense and varied field. The thoughtful reader finds himself engaged, during every waking moment he can spare for books and periodicals, by some embodiment or interpretation of life which has imaginative value, appealing to his higher curiosity and to his most widely varied tastes. His newspaper is not merely a chronicle; it charges the day's doings with their meaning and tendency, investing incident and circumstance with the guise of fancy and humor; even the reporter—who may be a budding novelist —does not fail of the picture; and well-equipped critics disclose with varying degree of charm the freshly emergent novelties in science, literature, society, art, and even archæology. His magazines, of which there are so many, and so many that are good, deepen the best of these satisfactions and offer him, in fiction and essay, a store of imaginative literature, richer, more diversified, and of a higher order than was ever before thus current in the world. In books, the whole treasury of human literature is at his command, and so much of the best of it is of his own generation that he will find in this alone the full complement of his culture, including the truest interpretation of the past.

All this is literature with the stamp of imagination upon it. Very little of it that is contemporary will ever meet the eyes of a future generation. The eminent writers of the past who have won immortality did not strive for it; they were helped to it through features which our writers have missed or repudiated—impressive accessories, association with heroic or religious themes, and, in times when there were few authors of any note, a singular assurance of prosperity with many generations. Their intrinsic excellence, which is undisputed, while an indispensable condition to lasting fame, would not alone have sufficed to save them from oblivion.

Our writers, unconsciously, it is true, but perseveringly, court evanescence. That is the course of evolution in Nature. The inorganic endures, but all living things pass, and return only in their successors. Never the same harvest blooms again. As literature comes nearer to life it partakes more of its evanescence, which, in the case of humanity, is more pronounced than it is in Nature. This comparative disadvantage, as it seemed to our predecessors, found a partial compensation in the durable monuments of art. But we do not look upon it as such a disadvantage, and instead of seeking durability we are not only inclined but compelled to promote mutation and expedite the passing.

The word "duration" suggests hardness, immovable permanence, the stability of Cathay. Men were used to think of eternity as endless duration. Now we have come to think of it as a quality of the psychical life. Water wears away and outwears the rock. Only that which freely flows, which is mobile, quick in change and passage, can have real stability. Our modern conservatism is not a clinging to old modes, a plea for stereotyped fashions; it is rather a plea for time—however brief the moment—in which to change. The obstinacy of the old conservatism, a protest against mutation, insured the ruin, through brittleness or rot, of all it sought to preserve, leading the way to precisely the same meaningless dust or refuse that iconoclasm leaves in its wake. Iconoclasm, therefore, belongs wholly to the past—to those periods in which its precipitate corrosions were invited; in our day the general sense waits upon conservatism and deprecates destruction of values. The stability of our civilization is secured by those mutations which are a distinctive feature of modern constructive organization. The destruction of values by war is coming to be looked upon as an intolerable barbarism.

To expedite the passing is the law of our modern life. We reinforce all sane and wholesome currents, all that are not impelled by rages and hatreds, and in time shall thus prevent the waste and futility of attempts to sustain decrepitudes. Even in our pathology we stimulate fevers and send after disease its own specific virus or, what is better, preveniently anticipate it by the same means — so clearing the stream.

It is a fortunate era we have reached, when we are no longer, as Sir Thomas Browne said, "Januses of one face," and that face turned ever to the past. The forward look has so gained upon us that all of our old men who have been really modern find in the imagination of things to come a charm outvying that of retrovision. Our imagination shows more creative power in its prophetic office than when its commerce was with the past, trafficking with memories and memorials.

The charm which holds us lies in what is becoming, in a life unfolding itself and seen in its own light; and for our generation the ever-fresh disclosures have a potent spell, leading us on in new paths. Our imagination does not feed alone upon the enshrined show-bread of memory.

It is not a formless, colorless, or flavorless world which furnishes the rich content of this freshly awakened human sensibility in our time. We are held to the perceptions and impressions of the present, finding such satisfaction in our real sense of these that we do not need to revert to some older bond established by association for a reinforcement of our interest, rather indeed waiting for what is next to come, to heighten the charm. For it is a flowing, ever-changing world. It always was this, but we have become, ourselves, so responsively fluent that the novelty and the surprise no longer escape us; and out of these changes in us has come a new humanity, with novelties and surprises of transcendent interest.

This eagerly waiting attitude of ours does not incline us to visit old crypts and dusty chambers to look upon memorials and effigies; and it does dispose us with genuine psychical hospitality to

"Welcome the coming, speed the parting guest."

Surely there was some sad lack of imagination betrayed in the former so general habit of looking upon the present as flat and stale simply because it was modern. Rather, with Faust, we should count that moment happy which we bid to stay, and better still—better for our faith in life—when we are willing that any moment, however happy, should pass, sure of the more bountiful sequel. We have become lovers of change, not from the nomadic impulse bred in the desert, and not for the sake of variety so much as for our interest in the variation which forever discloses new values—values which even in that old dark article of death shine so brightly that we are more interested than appalled by what seems to us but a new and vastly more revelatory turn of the shifting curtain.

All of our life which has for us beauty, interest, and meaning is made up of evanescences, of things that are passing and which we willingly let pass. This is as true of past generations as of our own, and those generations found in the shifting scenes and situations a by no means stinted share of human delights and satisfactions; but for us the phenomena are different. Life, so generous for them, is yet for us far more abundant and varied in its bounty, and we have quite another perspective of its real values. They were more exacting, formal, and tenacious in the outward conduct of life, and more jealously guarded a visible integrity. We have more faith in life, confident of its inward harmony, and let it freely flow, seeking its own levels; we are not afraid of inconsistency, and readily give up the outward for an invisible integrity. We are sure of our harmony and do not strain to keep it at high pitch; chaos will not ensue upon our relaxation. Ours is not the burden of Atlas. Souls will not be lost for lack of our inquisition. Yet the currents of the world's life, thus freely flowing, are strong enough for their own issues and for the salvation of all who yield to them. Response to the truth is more important than that old mistaken sense of responsibility to which more than half of the almost unthinkable cruelties of the past were due.

Literature as well as life has been released from an unnatural strain through our new sense of values. Walls are for the garden, not the garden for walls; and our real life, certainly our real literature, is wholly concerned with the garden and with its living and evanescent flowers and fruits. Formerly the imagination dwelt in the house of Fame, exalting

heroic or saintly deeds and personalities; now it is
not busy with things that are memorable or monu-
mentally lasting; it dwells in the house of Life.
The phenomena which appeal to it and which engage its powers do not crystallize in fixed external
features or traits, are always in flux and have no
permanence, are, therefore, not matters of record
or memorial, but, being moments of mind and heart
or, at their firmest, moods that take shapes as clouds
do in the sky, have no statics and are caught only
in passing. Such moments or moods have, in all
times, made the best part of human life—the very
life of life—but not the best on the same psychical
plane as ours, and, therefore, not having the same
high esteem in critical appreciation or in imaginative
selection. The values which our present generation
most cherishes in literature have not distinguished
the literature and, still less, the art of former ages.

Even in our interpretation of the past we seek,
as far as possible, to get back of the memorial, back
of those things which formerly seemed most worthy
of record, and so made up the body of human history;
yet if we were successful, we should not find psychical phenomena of the same order as those which
abound in our modern life, and which have our
preference as imaginative motives because of their
higher interest and excitement—more than compensating those we have surrendered. If every
part of the world's life were brought within the full
operation of this dynamic psychical harmony, we

should have as reasonable a millennium as we could hope for—and should no longer make history, certainly not after the manner of former generations. Already we are puzzled how fitly to commemorate a three hundred years' old poet, we are so tired of outward monuments. For records shall we hereafter be obliged to content ourselves with those of commerce and industry and athletics, of the best sellers in the book market, of the speed of automobiles and ocean liners, the flights of air-ships, and the long-windedness of congressional speechmakers, or of the applause given to presidential candidates in political conventions? All these are fluctuating enough to meet the modern note of change and of absolute contemporaneity, but have no psychical significance and no imaginative value; they belong to the mere routine of journalism.

Each new generation suffices more and more for itself, and, whatever regard it may have for antiquity, it has little for an invisible posterity—none at all for any glory that posterity may confer upon it. It is faithfully reflected in its imaginative literature —in that portion of it which is either an interpretation or representation of contemporary life. What matter if the next generation, in its own self-sufficiency, is oblivious of the reflection, and treats this passing literature as in a palimpsest, writing its own above it?

There is another portion of literature in each generation, not so entirely contemporary in its aim, but, as in the case of Mrs. Humphry Ward's fiction, linking itself with the past, while wholly modern in its psychical method and meaning. We should say that modernity is with Mrs. Ward a passion, whatever the background of her work. This class of literature is especially important for its culture-values. Whether on that account it will last any longer is by no means certain. It may be that we have reached the time when even the torch-bearers are illuminated only by the passing flame.

But there remains still another kind of imaginative literature—a more unconscious, indeed an absolutely spontaneous, manifestation of genius, and more distinctively creative than any other. In our day it is sure to be fiction, and just because it is so purely creative it is profoundly and inevitably interpretative. We speak of it as if it were actually in evidence, but we should rather say that there are in certain works of fiction of our time, beginning with the early novels of Thomas Hardy, indications of it, samples showing its kind rather than works fully illustrating its possibilities. Thus we have in one writer a native quaintness of characterization which has fascinated European as well as American readers, but lacking in might of thought or feeling; in another, might enough of humor and fancy to have made his name known in the most secluded nook of Christendom; in another, the power beyond any one in her generation to create living men and women; in another, just beginning her career, a plain portraiture which sometimes seems like a bravura of realism; and in still another, this realistic representation made especially significant by a subtle imagination. In all the work coming within the class now under consideration perhaps that of Thomas Hardy and Mark Twain comes nearest to a large and significant realization of the possibilities of the new literature.

This kind of imaginative creation we do not associate with culture-values. It is all modern—could indeed only spring up in our time; but we do not look upon the creators of it as passing on the torch—they have no place in that light-bearing procession. When we read Conrad's *Lord Jim* or Kenneth Grahame's *Golden Age*, we do not give them a definite place in the course of human culture, as we do the writings of Thackeray, George Eliot, Mrs. Humphry Ward, and Henry James. This kind of work seems, in a way, almost dateless, as Mrs. Mary Wilkins Freeman's stories seem.

If we are to be surprised by some new Immortal, he will come in this dateless fashion, like a Melchisedec, "without generation or length of days." And we are, not altogether without hope, looking for him, or, it may as well be, for her. This coming author will be a modern of the moderns—it is only thus that he can surprise his contemporaries, ourselves or those who come after us. His genius may remind us of the greatest of the old Immortals—of Shakespeare or, as Hardy's did when it first dawned upon us, of the Greek masters of tragedy; but it will not come in the guise of any of these. He will not be compared as to excellence with writers past or present so that criticism can point out that in this or that respect he is in the advance. He will not be praised for his subtle analysis or his exquisite art. Without any of the tricks of the showman, any theatrical poses or effects, or any such masterfulness as will lose him the reader's intimacy, he will have the large appeal and be popular.

We cannot give away the secret of such an author's charm, or combination of charms, since he is to be a surprise, the Unprecedented, dealing with the unprecedented phenomena of the new world which his creative and interpretative imagination shall discover. Psychical phenomena, surely—that way must lie the supreme excitement, play, humor, and enchantment.

In the mean time—that is, while we are still awaiting the emergence of a genius which shall fully illustrate the possibilities that we hopelessly attempt to define—we must listen to the tiresome complaint of the mediocrity of contemporary literature.

Every modern advantage which we may reasonably consider an excellence, as indicating an advance in our departure from the life and literature of the past, seems to involve just that kind of disadvantage which makes for mediocrity. We might therefore infer that mediocrity itself is the distinctive excellence of modernity. And such it is negatively—

that is, as precluding certain kinds of superiority. But it has only this negative virtue. Mediocrity invites disaster to literature and to every other human interest not sordidly material. Our hope is in our belief that the mediocrity characterizes only the outward fashions of our life; that the appearance of a dead level is due only to the absence of the kind of eminences which we have repudiated; that some new psychical sovereignty or compulsion— more native to life, more vitally uplifting and significant—has displaced that mock show of mastery which, in the past, has proved wholly inadequate to a full realization of humanity.

The manifestation of this less obvious but only real aristocracy seems to us to be shown in our life and in our literature. But there is room for its more buoyant expression, for the ampler expansion of its power—such as shall expel the word "mediocrity" from the critic's vocabulary. This consummation cannot be reached in our fiction—and it is there that it must be realized—by *finesse* of art or any masterful legerdemain of treatment, by study or by mental or emotional stress, and, least of all, by reversion to old methods and motives. It may come, as we have intimated, through some exceptional genius which will give to our era such distinction as Shakespeare gave the Elizabethan and Dickens the Victorian; or a group of writers may emerge, each in his separate and distinct eminence, whose genius shall fully illustrate the imaginative values of the new order with such creative power as shall bring on the Summer of our literature, in its glowing light and brooding heat; its expanse and abundance as well as variety and free play under loftier skies; its natural excess, through reinforcement without exaggeration — showing that a psychical realism involves supreme excitement and passion; dramatic movement without theatrical show; the art which nature makes; the pulsation, vibrancy, and full volume of life.

We are not confessing to the weakness of our new literature, which we do not regard as either mediocre or anæmic, though we are looking for better examples of its strength. Probably the complaining critic might more justly be brought to the confessional, so blind does he seem to values not meeting expectations based on an old habit of judgment. Criticism is apt to lag far behind creative power, as it did in the days of Jeffrey and Keats. Ours is not a period of transition, in respect of the attitude of the imaginative writer, but one of waiting for his mightiest achievement.

# INDEX

ABBEY, EDWIN A., art of, 51, 270.

Adams, John Quincy, his impressions of European travel contributed to Dennie's *Portfolio*, 43.

Adams, Phineas, founder of the Anthology Club, Boston, 43.

Addison, Joseph, contributor to the *Tatler*, *Spectator*, and *Guardian*, 9; effect upon his generation of his appreciation of Milton, 10; Dr. Johnson's tribute to his style, 18.

*Adventurer*, the, established by Dr. Hawkesworth and contributed to by Dr. Johnson, 18.

Ainsworth, Harrison, novels of, in *Bentley's Miscellany*, with illustrations by Cruikshank, 36.

Akenside, Dr. Mark, first poems of, in the *Gentleman's Magazine*, 28; Hazlitt's comparison of, with Wordsworth, 28.

Aldrich, Thomas Bailey, contributor to New York *Home Journal*, 47; editor of the *Atlantic Monthly*, 52.

Alison, Sir Archibald, contributor to *Blackwood's*, 34.

Allingham, William, associated with James Anthony Froude in editorship of *Fraser's*, and his successor, 37.

*American Whig Review*, Poe's "Raven" contributed to, but first published, by permission, in the New York *Mirror*, 46.

*Analectic Magazine*, Moses Thomas's, edited by Washington Irving, 43.

Anonymity: to old-time audiences the author's individuality of no serious concern, 80; reasons for masked authorship in the eighteenth century, 81, 82; "Mr. Bickerstaff" in the *Spectator*, 81; "Junius," 82; author of "Ossian," 82; forgeries of Chatterton, 82; nineteenth century pseudonyms: the "Waverley" disguise, "Boz," and "George Eliot," 83; lapse of Bulwer to anonymity after he had won distinction, 83; advantages of anonymity to new author, 84; "Elia," a warm cloak for Charles Lamb, 84; difference formerly between the esteem for books and that for periodical contributions, 85; Lockhart's unpleasant associations with magazines, culminating in the fate of John Scott, 85; disclosure of names would have revealed the poverty of literature in the early nineteenth century, 85, 86;

# INDEX

of eighteenth century, to actual life, 24, 25; excluded from eighteenth-century periodicals, 25; serial publication of Smollett's *Sir Lancelot Greaves* an exception, 26; Walpole, Mrs. Radcliffe, 26; development of fiction after 1850, 53, 54; supreme interest of, psychical, 67; evil in, 68; effect of the novel and the periodical on literature, 111; popularity desirable, 121–132; narrow appeal of some of our best novelists, 121–129; novelist's own fault if he has not the mastery of popular thought and feeling, 129; excessive reserve, 129; great masters of the past had the excellence of their defects—those of the present too much the defects of their excellences, 132; comparative estimates of different periods often misleading, 135; the course of Greek imaginative literature, 135, 136; every advance in evolution involves sacrifice of elemental force for structural excellence, 137; individualistic development, 138; the eclipses and revivals of certain individual writers at different periods, 138; our own age the only one having a clear and complete retrospect, 139; the present, while appreciating, excludes the past, 139, 140; style cannot pass from age to age and still seem native to the time, 141; our development largely on the side of our sensibility, 141; our satisfaction with past masterpieces precludes their repetition, 142; authors illustrating modern realism, 143; enlarged scope of realistic fiction, 143–153; main current of English fiction of the last century, domestic and social, 155; greater flexile ingenuity of the novelist, combining the masteries of the other arts, also his peril, 170, 171; nothing denied to fiction which is of human concern, 172, 173; backgrounds of novels sometimes more interesting than the dramatic situations, as in Hichens's *Garden of Allah*, 176; the greater the mastery of subjective psychical phenomena in a novel, the greater the need of extension of its world affiliations, 176; our departure from the Victorian era, 178–181; examples of the new fiction in novels and short stories, 179, 180; Thomas Hardy and George Meredith prophets of the new order, 180; our writers not greater than the old, but in the advance, and appeal to an advanced sensibility, 181; the new sensibility a sensibility to reality, 197; a new kind of realism, 197; the passing of problem fiction, 200; of satire, 201; available values of fallibility as in Miss Sinclair's *The Helpmate*, 202; the change in love-stories, 203; in the treatment of primary relations, 204; real men and women take the place of villains and saints, 205; departure from old forms and mannerisms, 228; Blackmore, James, and Meredith, 228; class prejudice undermined by modern fiction, 236,

# INDEX

Jenyns, Soame, contributor to the *World*, 22.

Johnson, Dr. Samuel, teacher at Lichfield, 12; goes to London with Garrick, 12; association of, with the *Gentleman's Magazine*, 13; reporter of "Parliamentary Debates," 13; his didacticism, 15; personal and mental characteristics, 16; dictator in literary circles, 16; violently weak preceptor and critic, 17; his most characteristic writing in the *Rambler*, 18; contributions to the *Adventurer*, 18; tribute to Addison's style, 18; completion of Dictionary, 19; his afternoon levées, 19; not a successful humorist, 19; his *Idler*, contributed to also by Sir Joshua Reynolds and Bennet Langton, 19; his projected *Bibliothèque*, 20; association with the *Literary Magazine*; his *Rasselas*, 21, 96; pension from George III., 21; his death in 1784, 21.

"Junius," letters of, in the *Public Advertiser*, 39.

Kinglake, A. W., contributor to *Blackwood's Magazine*, 34.

Kingsley, Charles, his "Water Babies" published in *Macmillan's Magazine*, 38.

Kinship, earliest bond, 211, 212; the new psychical sense of, 226, 265.

*Knickerbocker Magazine*, the, Charles Fenno Hoffman first editor of, 48; contributed to by Hawthorne, Irving, and nearly every important writer of its time, 48; Longfellow's "Psalm of Life" first appeared in, anonymously, 48.

Lamb, Charles, his "Elia" essays in the *London Magazine*, 29; his love of antiquity, 116, 233.

Landor, Walter Savage, a contributor to *Blackwood's*, 34.

Langton, Bennet, friend of Dr. Johnson and contributor to his *Idler*, 19.

Lever, Charles, contributions of, to *Blackwood's Magazine*, 34.

*Liberal*, the, planned by Byron, Shelley, and Leigh Hunt, edited by Hunt, 30; Byron's "Vision of Judgment" opening the first number, 30.

*Literary Magazine*, Dr. Johnson's association with, 21.

*Literary Magazine*, Philadelphia, established by Charles Brockden Brown, 43.

Literature, reasons for late development of, in America, 50; quick sensibility to best English, in America, 50, 101; successive styles in the evolution of, for two centuries, first registered in the periodical, 55; the American audience, 56–68, 79; justification of new literary styles, 51, 57; deterioration of literature by New England matrons complained against by Mrs. Peattie, 55, 66; new spirit manifested in California and the Middle West, 57–67; feminism of culture, especially evident in the Middle West and on the Pacific coast, 58, 64—a modern characteristic everywhere in America and England, 63; contrary conditions in California thirty years ago, 58; modern literature confronts the truth of life, 67; reaction against and recurrence of the ele-

ter Scott, **20**; under Gifford's editorship, **29**; edited by Lockhart, **33**.

Longfellow, Henry W., contributions of, to *North American Review*, **44**; his "Spanish Student" in *Graham's Magazine*, **45**; his poem, "The Psalm of Life," first published anonymously in the *Knickerbocker Magazine*, **48**.

*Lounger*, the, succeeding the *Mirror* (Edinburgh), contributed to by Henry Mackenzie, **22**.

Lover, Samuel, editor of *Dublin University Magazine*, **35**.

Lowell, James Russell, editor of *North American Review*, **44**; starts the *Pioneer*, **47**; editor of the *Atlantic Monthly*, **52**.

MACAULAY, THOMAS BABINGTON, essays in *Edinburgh Review*, first published in book form in America, **101**.

Mackenzie, Henry, contributor to Edinburgh *Mirror* and *Lounger*, **22**.

*Macmillan's Magazine*, **37**.

Magazine, the monthly: first example of successful, the *Gentleman's Magazine*, **12**; emergence of, together with the novel, **14**; helped to abolish pedantry and secure independence of writers, **14**; the *London Magazine*, rival to the *Gentleman's Magazine*, **21**; the *Scots Magazine*, continued as the *Edinburgh Magazine*, **21**; the (new) *London Magazine*, **29**; Colburn's *New Monthly*, **29**; the *Metropolitan*, **29**; *Blackwood's*, **31**; *Bentley's Miscellany*, **36**; the *Monthly Magazine*, with Dickens's first story (1833), **36**; *Fra-*

*ser's* **36**; *Cornhill*, **36**; *Macmillan's Magazine*, **37**. American: Dennie's *Portfolio*, **43**; Charles Brockden Brown's *Literary Magazine*, **43**; Moses Thomas's *Analectic Magazine*, **43**; *Graham's Magazine*, **45**; New York *Monthly Review*, **46**; the *Broadway Journal*, **47**; the *New England Magazine*, **47**; the *Southern Literary Messenger*, **46**; Lowell's *Pioneer*, **47**; *Harper's Magazine* and the *Atlantic Monthly*, **49**; under pledge to exclude improprieties, **68**; scope of a first-class American magazine, **69–79**; educational function diminishing, **69**; may exclude specialties and even timely topics, **69**; principle of selection—the near and intimate note preferred—the theme of human interest, **70**; recent prominence of nature sketches, **71**; summation of features outside of fiction, **71**, **72**; fiction often serves the purpose of essays and articles in interpretation of life past and present, **72**; the same quality of excellence in magazines as in books, **72**; the elemental not excluded, but most effectively treated by the best writers, **77**; accommodation not expected of contributors, **78**; what the magazine has done for writers and artists, **79**; advantages of anonymity and the justification of its abandonment, **80–92**; peril to magazine literature from placing the name of the writer before the real value of his contribution, **88**, **89**; appreciation of the new and unknown

# INDEX

ence of, 11; copied entire by Elizabeth Montagu, 11; circulation of, 13.

*Spectator*, the, London literary weekly (1828), 13.

Steele, Sir Richard, contributor to the *Tatler*, *Spectator*, and *Guardian*, 9; started the *Tatler*, 12.

Sterling, John, associated with F. D. Maurice in editorship of the *Athenæum*, 23.

Sterne, Laurence, mock sentiment of, 23.

Stephen, Sir Leslie, editor of *Cornhill*, 36.

Stevenson, Louis, contributor to *Cornhill*, 36; to *Macmillan's Magazine*, 38.

Story, William Wetmore, contributor to the *Atlantic Monthly* and *Blackwood's*, 35.

Study, life does not yield itself to, 237; dulls sensibility and leads to loose thinking and shallow feeling, 238; the diagrammatic habit, 238.

Swift, as a pamphleteer, 7; his connection with the *Examiner*, 7; contributor to the *Spectator*, 9.

Talfourd, Sir Thomas, contributor to *London Magazine*, 29.

*Tatler*, the, 9, 10, 12.

Tennyson, Alfred, his "Lucretius" published in *Macmillan's*, 38.

Thackeray, William Makepeace, early offerings declined by *Blackwood's Magazine*, in which he never published, 35; contributor to *Fraser's*, 36; editor of *Cornhill*, 36; literary critic of the *Times*, 40; contributor to N. P. Willis's New York *Corsair*, 47; pay-

ments to, in *Fraser's*, 107; his *Yellowplush Papers*, first published in book-form in America, 258.

Thirteenth century, wonderful achievements of, 224; contest between Pope and Emperor, 224.

Thomson, James, his *Seasons*, serial after book publication of, 8.

*Times*, London, editorship of, offered to Tom Moore and to Southey, 40; Laurence Oliphant and Richard Monckton Milnes regular correspondents of, 40; Thackeray literary critic of, 40.

*Token*, the, annual, published by S. G. Goodrich ("Peter Parley"), contributed to by Bryant and Hawthorne, 46; edited in 1829 by N. P. Willis, 47.

Trevelyan, Sir George, his "The Competition Wallah," in *Macmillan's Magazine*, 38.

*Tribune*, New York, Margaret Fuller contributor to, 41.

Trollope, Anthony, active in the establishment of the *Fortnightly Review*, 37; contributor to *Macmillan's*, 38.

United States Literary Gazette, Boston, Bryant's poems in, 46.

Urbanity, the modern, 248–259.

Walpole, Horace, contributor to the *World*, 22; inclination to mediævalism, 25; prophetic characterization of the nineteenth century, 27.

War, now denounced by the world sense, once the vehicle of social organization, 223.

# INDEX

THE END